Advanced Embroidery Techniques

Advanced Embroidery Techniques

Beryl Johnson

B.T. Batsford Ltd · London

Acknowledgements

I wish most sincerely to thank my daughter, Lorna Powell, for her conscientious and unfailing help these past years. I sincerely thank Brian Melhuish, the photographer, for his patience and perseverance in producing the photographs for this book. To my husband I say thank you for all the years of help given by him, also to my daughter, Karen Melhuish, and to George Powell and Margaret Wildman, for their patience. They all helped to make the book possible.

First published 1983
© Beryl Johnson 1983

ISBN 0 7134 0085 4

Filmset by Servis Filmsetting Ltd, Manchester
Printed in Great Britain by
Butler & Tanner Ltd, Frome, Somerset
for the publishers,
B.T. Batsford Ltd,
4 Fitzhardinge Street, London, W1H 0AH

Contents

DOMESTIC MACHINES

TAMBOUR EMBROIDERY

Colour photographs

Introduction

I believe embroidery is created for a purpose, primarily to enhance a fabric; whether the fabric is used for a garment, a panel or for household use is the decision of the designer. This is by no means a modern idea, as both uses of embroidery have a long history, not only in England but also worldwide. In the past embroideries all had to be worked by hand, taking many hours to execute. The difference now is that the needlewoman has the choice between hand or machine work or a combination of both methods. I will always enjoy hand embroidery; however, in a modern age I also enjoy the variety of making embroidery with modern methods.

The Cornely and Irish machines are not very modern by today's standards; they have been used in industry since the nineteenth century. In all these years of use their original design has not been improved upon. There is no machine today that will work the various stitches of the Cornely. The Schiffli machine will work yards of embroidery in a satin stitch; the multi-head machines will produce more than one piece of embroidery at one time. These two are necessary for mass production, but these big machines cannot give the individuality and versatility that the designer can obtain when using the Cornely and Irish.

Tambour has also been used for many years, not only in industry but also by the individual. Today it still remains a very quick method of producing thread and beadwork; as yet no machine has been invented that can master the beadwork.

Patience and perseverance are the two most important virtues when approaching a subject for the first time. The machines will need co-ordination of the speed and the hand movement; if the machine speed is too fast then the hand control could prove difficult to master when you are using the machine for the first time. The tambour movement must be very precise to ensure complete control of the work.

I have tried to explain the techniques of each method in this book. It is a firm belief of mine that if you understand the techniques of what you are doing it will be easier to use each method to its fullest potential. This applies to each individual, whether you are at home teaching yourself, learning on a part time course or taking a full time course at a college. A person who can master each technique will add another valuable method to their vocabulary of embroidery. These methods must never be viewed in isolation, for a person who can experiment with them can produce endless variations to enhance any piece of work.

Cornely

1. Cornely L3 and LG3

These machines have great precision and are unique for the embroidery that can be produced on them. They have been used for many years and are today being used by various firms to produce embroidery for fashion and household articles.

The Cornely has a hook needle which produces the basic chain stitch. This chain stitch can be used for chain embroidery; it is also a holding stitch for seven other stitches worked by this machine. The moss stitch is the one exception, because this produces a series of loops, giving a raised pile effect. Therefore nine different stitches can be worked, but the permutations of these stitches are endless by the use of different threads, varying the amount of threads used and adjustments to the tension.

There is a rotary handle underneath the machine which enables the very free movements to be made with ease. It will work in any direction without turning the fabric round.

Most fabrics can be used on this machine, but a close woven nylon can be difficult although a soft nylon may work quite well. It is advisable always to try a sample. If it is found that the needle pulls the threads of the fabric, it may very well be because the needle is blunt and needs changing. These needles are made in short, medium and long points; the short and medium are the most used as the long point can prove a hindrance.

It is advisable to have a design on the fabric and so follow the line. The design should be as continuous as possible to avoid having too many finishing ends, as these ends must be finished off quite securely. If not, all the embroidery will unravel from the fabric. However, there are many designs that are usually worked freehand, without any design and with a continuous line. They can form a straight line or an allover pattern such as shell, vermicelli, bubble, curls or pinnacle, to name but a few.

Figure 1 (a) Freehand continuous design: (from left) Shell; Vermicelli; Bubble; Pinnacle

  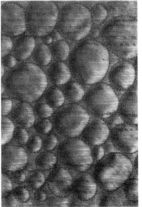 

The two cord, retard, three cord, pad, ribbon, braid and whip stitches are all worked with the aid of the machine attachments. These attachments are fitted onto the machine by the person using the machine, not by a mechanic. Any adjustments to the tensions for a correct working stitch must also be made by the person using the machine. The carrier tension will need adjustment while working, a tighter tension when the bobbin is full, a looser tension as threads are used and the bobbin becomes empty. It will therefore take time, practice and patience to understand and gain a good working knowledge of this machine. It is best to gain this from working the basic chain stitch and then to move on to the more complex stitches.

If thought and understanding is given to the use of the Cornely it should not prove to be a great problem. This will mean that if the machine is not producing a correct stitch at the first attempt the stitch must be analysed to find out why, and then the correct adjustments can be made to rectify the fault. The Cornely can really only produce the stitches that the operator has adjusted it to produce.

For embroidery on the Cornely trace the design onto the right side of the fabric, as the embroidery is worked on the right side.

2. Operating the Machine

It is advisable to sit directly in front of the machine needle and the round pressure foot section of the machine. (Figure 1b). Push in the start button on the electric control box. This is usually found at the right-hand side of the table support. Place your feet on the foot plate and sit comfortably at the machine; some people prefer to use only one foot for this. Add downward pressure with the feet. This will result in the electric motor of the machine turning the top wheel only. This action is used for winding the cotton using the shaft, which will be referred to in a later chapter.

To start the machine working place the right hand on the crank handle located underneath the machine table. Pull down; this will then click. (Diagram 1). Let the weight of the hand hold the crank handle down. It is not necessary for this to be gripped very tightly; the weight of the hand is

Figure 1 (b) Cornely. Sit directly in front of the machine needle and the round pressure foot section of the machine

Diagram 1 The crank handle is pulled down and held down with the weight of the hand while working the Cornely

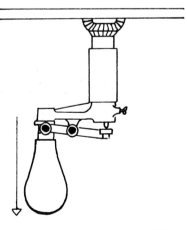

sufficient for this. Place your feet on the foot plate, then gently add downward pressure to control the speed for working the machine at a slow speed. The machine is now in operation. Release the crank handle first for this to stop. Using the machine this way – pulling the crank handle down first, and then adding pressure with the feet – it is much easier for the worker to control the speed and start of the working operation with this machine.

Hand Movement

The movement of the hand turning the crank handle in a circle or a square will be transmitted to the pressure foot movement. Draw a line of circles and a line of squares on a piece of felt fabric such as Vilene. (Diagram 2). Place this fabric underneath the pressure foot with the needle directly over the beginning of the first line. Lower the pressure foot by the lever located at the back of the machine. (Diagram 3). Start the machine motor, pull down the crank handle, add pressure to the foot plate to control the speed at slow to begin with and turn the crank handle to follow the design line. You must read the design with your eyes and co-ordinate what is seen with the hand movement, and keep to the design line. This perfect manipulation of the crank handle plus co-ordination and speed of the machine can be mastered with practice and patience.

Any intricate design can be followed once the required skill has been mastered. The machine can also be worked at a very high speed. However, it should be kept in mind that the person using the machine is in full command of the hand movement and the speed of the machine by the weight of pressure put on by the feet.

When the material is placed under the pressure foot it should be left in the same position; it is not necessary to turn the work round as with other machines. The left hand may be rested on the work to help steady and keep the material from turning in any direction. However, it should never be held so tight that the material is not left free for the pressure foot action to work, taking the material forward and back in co-ordination with the right hand movement.

Diagram 2 Co-ordinate the hand movement and follow the design line

Diagram 3 The pressure foot lever in the down position

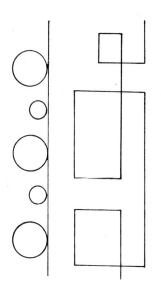
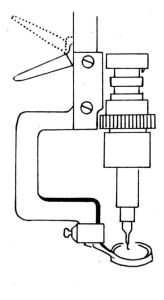

3. Chain Stitch

The chain stitch is achieved with a continuous thread coming from the underneath of the machine and a hook needle fitted in the needle bar. If different threads are used, then adjustments must be made to the machine for a satisfactory result. (Figures 1a, 2a, 2b, 2c).

Figure 2 (a) Chain stitch worked with a thick and fine cotton thread and a rayon twist

Figure 2 (b) Chain stitch used to construct an open fabric; the single chain lines are held in place by the solid areas of chain

15

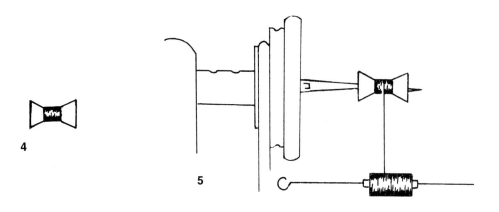

4

5

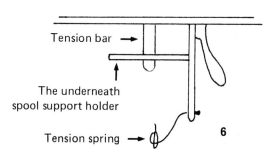

Tension bar →

The underneath
spool support holder

Tension spring → ⌀

6

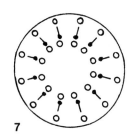

7

Diagram 4 The spool for the underneath thread must have the side shoulder edge

Diagram 5 The shoulder spool is pushed onto the shaft and wound even with the right hand while the thread is held on the winding wire

Diagram 6 The underneath spool holder; raise the tension bar to push the spool onto the support holder

Diagram 7 Push the threading wire through the hole that has the split coming to the outside of the round plate

Diagram 8 Place the thread in the threading wire with the left hand underneath. Pull the wire with the thread to the top with the right hand

Diagram 9 Pull the thread forward, with the hook knife underneath the pressure foot

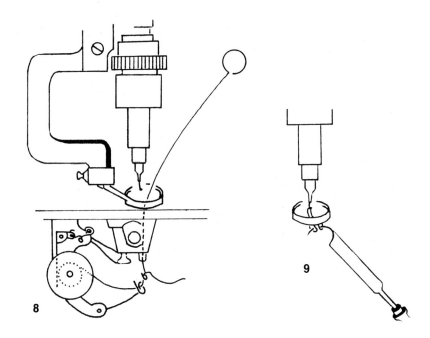

8

9

Chain Stitch Wind Spool

The spool used for this machine must be one that has shoulders or side edges. (Diagram 4). If the thread is on a straight card spool it must be wound onto a shoulder spool suitable for use. To do this, place the shoulder spool on the shaft located in the centre of the top wheel; this wheel always turns backwards. Hold the thread card spool on a winding wire – this is a straight piece of wire. Hold the winding wire in the left hand, guide the thread onto the shoulder spool with the right hand. Wind a little thread from the spool on the wire onto the top of the spool on the shaft; add pressure to the foot plate. (Diagram 5). This must be wound on smoothly and evenly to avoid an uneven chain stitch. This operation is quite speedy; it is not necessary to wind the whole thread from the spool onto the shoulder spool. Leave a little of the spool shoulders protruding above the smooth wound thread.

Threading the Machine

The reel holder is located underneath the machine at the back left. (Diagram 6). Raise the tension bar, push the spool onto the holder, then let the tension bar rest directly on the thread. The thread from the spool must run from the top of the spool; pass the thread through the loop in the tension spring, which is located in front of the reel holder.

Push the threading wire through the split hole in the round plate; this is in front of the needle hole. (Diagram 7). Push the threading wire from the top inside the round pressure foot to the underneath of the machine. (Diagram 8). Place the thread in the hook of the threading wire with the left hand and pull this through to the top of the round plate with the right hand. Pull the thread underneath the pressure foot to the front of the machine and hold this with the left hand. Pull down the crank handle sharply with the right hand, then take the right hand away, keep hold of the thread with the left hand and press down with the feet on the foot plate to work one stitch only.

The hook needle will pick up the thread through the needle hole in the plate. Pull the thread forward with the curved end of the hook knife passed underneath the pressure foot. (Diagram 9). The machine is now ready for working chain stitch on fabric. This is the only way to thread the machine. If at any time the machine refuses to work on fabric, re-thread the machine as described. If the stitch makes a drop stitch the thread may have escaped from the tension spring. If the thread will not pick up with the crank handle facing front, turn the crank handle to face 11 o'clock and pick up again.

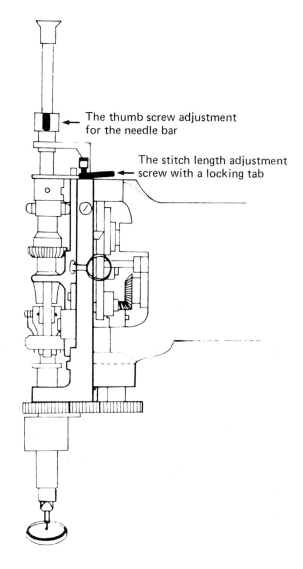

The thumb screw adjustment
for the needle bar

The stitch length adjustment
screw with a locking tab

Diagram 10 The three chain
stitch adjustments

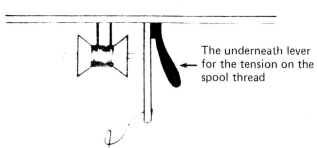

The underneath lever
for the tension on the
spool thread

Chain Stitch Adjustment

The stitch adjustments can be made three different ways.

1. *Thread tension*

Firstly, by the tension on the thread spool underneath the machine. The tension lever is located to the right of the spool holder. Pull this foward for a loose tension, back for a tight tension. This will regulate the flow of the cotton. (Diagram 10).

If this is too loose the result will be known as slipping; the stitch will show a series of loops, not connected chain stitch. If there is continual breaking the tension is too tight.

2. *Stitch lengths*

The stitch length is the amount of fabric pushed along by the pressure foot to make one stitch. At the top left-hand side of the machine will be found a screw with a locking tab. Knock the tab backwards with the handle of the hook knife. Turn the screw anti-clockwise to make the stitch length longer, screw clockwise to make the stitch length shorter. The tab must now be knocked forward to secure the length and hold it in its new position. (Diagram 10).

If this is not locked, the working vibration of the machine will work the screw loose, resulting in the stitch length getting longer. With a very long stitch length and a tight underneath tension the result will be a gathering of the fabric.

3. *Needle positions*

The needle position is described as being high, medium or low. For chain stitch make sure the hook of the needle is always facing the front of the machine. The front position is with the crank handle and the thumb screw on the needle bar facing forward. To adjust this height release the thumb screw on the needle bar by turning it to the left, adjust the height, then tighten the thumb screw on the needle bar to retain the position. (Diagram 10).

If the needle is too high the chain stitch will have large loops, if it is too low the chain will look like a straight line and the fabric will not have sufficient room to pass under the needle.

All three adjustments make a contribution to the achievement of good working chain stitch, and must all be remembered for the correction of a bad chain stitch. Check the threading as well, in case the thread has been caught up anywhere, making the tension feel too tight, and that the thread hasn't escaped from the tension spring, which would give a drop slip stitch.

Needle Size for the Different Threads

It is possible to produce quite a variation with the chain stitch by using different threads. A 50 thread will produce a fine chain, whereas a 2-ply wool or perlé will produce a heavy chain. (Figure 2c). However, this will necessitate changing the needle and the nipple; the needle must be selected with great care according to the thickness of thread. (Table I). When considering the embroidery that is going to be produced, the size of thread will be taken into account. It is always advisable to try the stitch on a spare piece of fabric before contemplating any embroidery.

Table I *Chain stitch variation*

Stitch	Needle size		Nipple size	Thread size	Tension size	Needle height	Length
	new	*old*					
small	90	3	3	50 thread	fairly tight	medium to low	small to medium
	100	4	4	rayon twist	medium	medium	medium
				fine metal thread	medium	medium	medium
medium	110	5	5	rayon floss	medium	medium to slightly high	medium to large
large	120	6	6	2-ply wool	loose	high	large
				Jap metal thread	loose	high	medium
large	130	7	7	perlé	loose	high	large
	140	8	8				

The thickness of the thread that is to be used will dominate the size of needle and nipple that should be used, as well as the size of the needle hole in the round machine plate; this must be able to accommodate the size of needle plus the thread being used.

Changing the Needle, Nipple and Plate

Needle

Release the thumb screw holding the needle bar and pull it straight up to remove the bar and needle. Hold the needle bar in the left hand and grip the needle with pliers in the right hand. (Figure 3). It is imperative while taking the needle out that the two must be kept in a straight line. If the

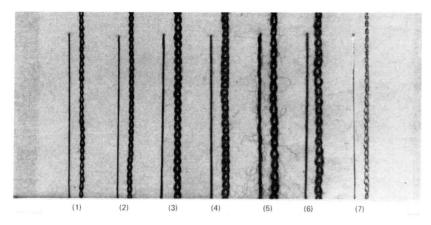

Figure 2 (c) Needle size for thread: (from left to right) (1) Small 50 fine thread; (2) Small rayon twist; (3) Medium rayon floss; (4) Large thick crochet thread; (5) Large 2-ply wool; (6) Large perlé; (7) Large jap metal thread

(1)   (2)   (3)   (4)   (5)   (6)   (7)

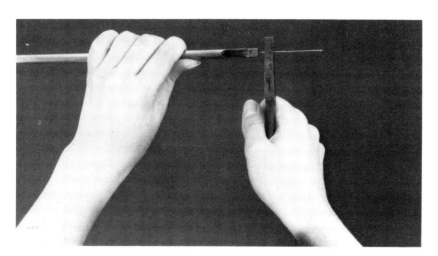

Figure 3 To remove the needle it is imperative that the needle bar and the needle should always be held in a straight line and never be forced to bend

needle bar or the needle is forced to bend by any slight action, the needle will break in the bar. (As a result, the needle bar would have to be sent away to have an engineer remove the thread section of the needle, and the machine would be out of action for quite some time unless there is a spare needle bar).

To take the needle out, turn the needle bar to the left, while holding the pliers tight on the needle; keep turning the bar until the needle thread section is free. To replace the needle, start the thread section off by hand, needle bar in the left hand, needle in the right hand. Make sure the needle is in securely, not forced in, by holding the needle with the pliers and turning the needle bar to the right. Again, make absolutely sure the two are held in a straight line to avoid it breaking. Replace the needle bar but do not put the needle right down in a working position.

Nipple

(Figure 4a). Place the small spanner around the top section of the nipple and turn the spanner to the left until the nipple is free. (Figure 4b). Replace the new nipple with the small spanner, turning to the right until secure.

Figure 4 (a) The nipple with its holder and screw (in pieces) and screwed into the nipple holder and the adjusting spanner

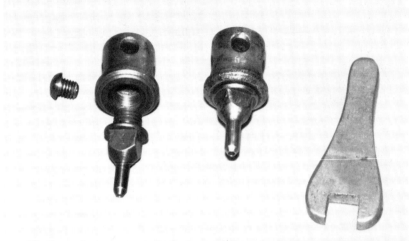

Figure 4 (b) Place the spanner around the top section of the nipple to turn

Plate

The round machine plate must have the right size hole selected to accommodate the needle size and the thread being used with ease.

The round machine plate is held in place by a screw from underneath. To change the hole locate the round solid screw head underneath the machine. This is in front of the spool holder section but to the back of the box. (Diagram 11). Grip the screw head with the right hand and turn to the left, just to release the round plate. Select the correct size hole for the needle and thread being used; this must be placed directly under the needle. The needle must be put down to go in the very centre of the hole so that there is free movement when the crank handle is turned round. Position the round plate to accommodate this; secure it in the correct position by turning the screw head to the right.

Position the needle to the thickness of thread that is being used; the needle must face the front of the machine. Thread the machine and try the stitch on a spare piece of fabric; make any stitch adjustment at this point to achieve a good standard chain stitch before commencing any embroidery.

Diagram 11 Box underneath

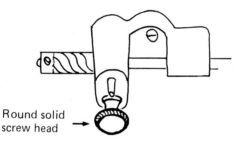

Round solid
screw head →

Fastening Off the Chain Stitch

After all the chain stitch design has been completed, the stitch must be fastened off.

To do this, release a little thread from the underneath spool with the left hand. Using the point of the curved section of the hook knife, pick up the thread from the needle and pull the loop forward. (Diagram 12). Cut the thread with the blade section of the hook knife. Raise the pressure foot and take the fabric out of the working position. The last chain stitch has been caught. The length of thread coming from the last stitch must be taken to the wrong side of the fabric with a needle, over the last loop; fasten off with a few stitches. If the chain stitch has not been finished off in this way the stitch will run back, as it is a continuous thread.

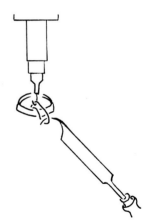

Diagram 12 Using the point of the hook knife, pull the thread forward

4. Shuttle

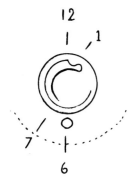

Diagram 13 Cut-out thread section showing clock face positions

Opposite

Diagram 14 Needle and shuttle movements for one chain stitch

1. Rest position
2. Shuttle forward, needle and nipple down
3. Shuttle forward, needle and nipple down further
4. Shuttle forward, needle only down
5. Shuttle forward, needle only down, holding the thread
6. Shuttle forward, needle down, holding the thread in place
7. Shuttle forward, needle down, holding the thread in place
8. Shuttle forward, needle only up, holding the thread
9. Shuttle back, needle only up, holding the thread
10. Shuttle back, nipple only up, thread held by the needle
11. Shuttle back, nipple up, thread held by the needle
12. Shuttle back to rest position, nipple up to complete one chain stitch

The shuttle position is important when using this machine. The shuttle is underneath the round machine plate beneath the pressure foot.

Shuttle Position

When setting the shuttle the positions of a clock face are used. Additionally, the position refers to the thread cut-out section, not to the end of the spiral. (Diagram 13). The shuttle position should be set between 12 and 1 o'clock for the chain stitch. To complete one chain stitch the shuttle needle and nipple movements can be seen in Diagram 14. At the completed stitch the nipple is in the highest position with the needle in the pre-set position.

Shuttle and Box

If the machine will not work a good chain stitch after making all the necessary adjustments, check the shuttle position.

To do this, remove pressure foot and plate, and first raise the needle bar using the top thumb screw. Remove the round pressure foot and locate the square holding link at the back of the foot. At the back of the link is the thumb screw which holds the foot in position. To release the thumb screw, sit at the front of the machine, place hands either side of the pressure foot and with both forefingers turn the thumb screw clockwise. (Figure 5). Two turns will be sufficient. Push down the square holding link and pull the foot slightly forwards and remove to the left. Remove the round machine plate, turn the solid screw head underneath the machine until it is free from the machine plate and push the screw upwards to raise and remove the plate.

The shuttle is now visible. The crank handle must be facing the front; turn the top wheel backwards to make sure the previous stitch has been completed. Check the shuttle position to make sure it is between 12 and 1 o'clock.

Lifting the machine

If a correction is to be made, turn the crank handle to face the back. Release the holding keys underneath the machine at the centre front and back by turning these in line with the edge of the machine base. Release the leather belt and pull it to the left with the left thumb while turning the top wheel back with the right hand. This will feed off the leather belt from

24

Diagram 14 Needle and shuttle movements for one chain stitch

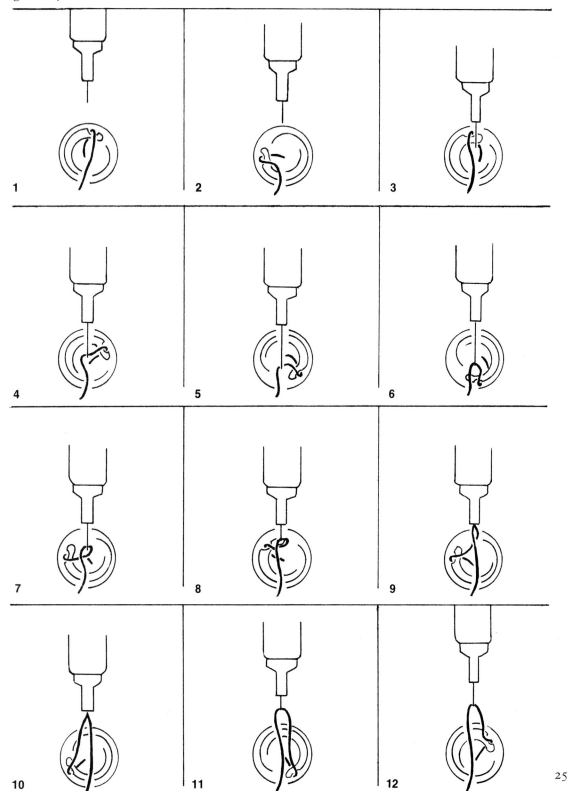

1

2

3

4

5

6

7

8

9

10

11

12

25

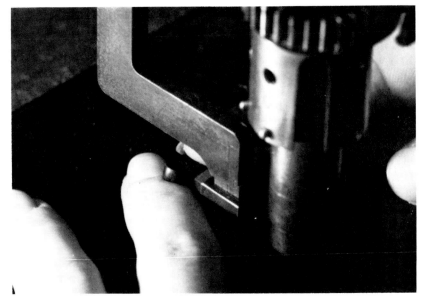

Figure 5 Removing the pressure foot. Place hands either side of the pressure foot; with both forefingers turn the thumb screw clockwise

Figure 6 (a) The crank handle turned directly forward to rest on the table top. The underneath box is now visible

Underneath box

the groove of the top wheel. Release the leather belt from the lower wheel underneath the machine, then with the right hand lift the leather belt right over the top wheel to the right. The machine is now free; tip the machine backwards by pushing the top section back until the crank handle is above the table top. Turn the crank handle directly forward and rest this on the table top. The underneath box is visible. (Figure 6a). This has a straight rod to the right connected to the cogs at the back of the crank handle.

To the left of the box there is a straight cog with a screw facing to the front. To complete one stitch, this straight cog (being connected to the lower thread cog section of the shuttle) passes to the right, going part way through the box, thus making half the shuttle movement. It then comes back to the left to complete the shuttle movement.

Shuttle Adjustment

Make a note of the shuttle position; has it to be advanced or set back?

To adjust the shuttle, release the front screw with a screwdriver and hold a piece of fabric behind the screw on the straight cog. Never take the screw right out. As the straight cog is pulled to the left, the shuttle will

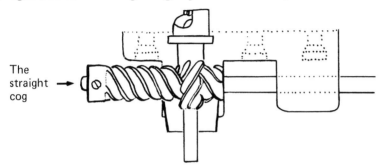

The
straight →
cog

Diagram 15 Cog section of shuttle

Figure 6 (b) Two important points are: (1) the screw must face the front; (2) the straight cog must never protrude on the right side of the box

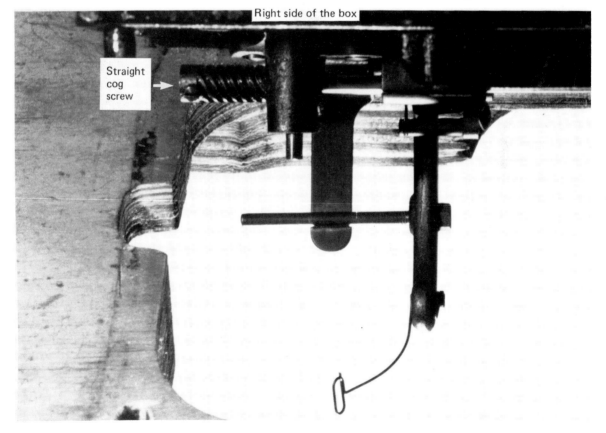

Right side of the box

Straight
cog →
screw

turn to the left. At this stage the shuttle is advanced or set back, by turning the lower section of the shuttle with the right hand. Push the straight cog back into the box, connecting this with the cog section of the shuttle. (Diagram 15). The shuttle must rest between 12 and 1 o'clock, with the straight cog screw facing front. The right-hand side of the straight cog must never protrude from the right-hand side of the box. (If the straight cog is set in a protruding position the machine will be unable to complete one stitch). The two cogs will slide easily into each other; with a little practice the correct position will be located.

Two things are very important: the screw must face the front; the straight cog must never protrude from the right side of the box. (Figure 6b). Hold a piece of fabric behind the screw in the left hand, with the correct location of the shuttle, and secure the screw tightly with the screwdriver.

Tip the machine back as before, to lower the machine, turn the crank handle to the back and lower the machine into the table. Bring the leather strap back over the top wheel, replace the strap onto the lower wheel and then onto the top wheel. Work the machine to make sure the shuttle has retained its position; if it has moved, follow the instructions again to re-set the shuttle. If it is satisfactory, replace and secure the round machine plate with the needle in the centre of the hole, replace and secure the pressure foot, lower the needle to working position and tighten the holding keys underneath the machine. Re-thread the machine and work a sample of the stitch to make sure it is working perfectly.

5.   Moss Stitch

The appearance of moss stitch is a raised pile, loop stitch, similar to towelling, sometimes known as carpet stitch. (Figure 7).

Shuttle Change

Refer to the section on shuttle adjustment in the previous chapter; the same movement must be made with the straight cog but the shuttle must

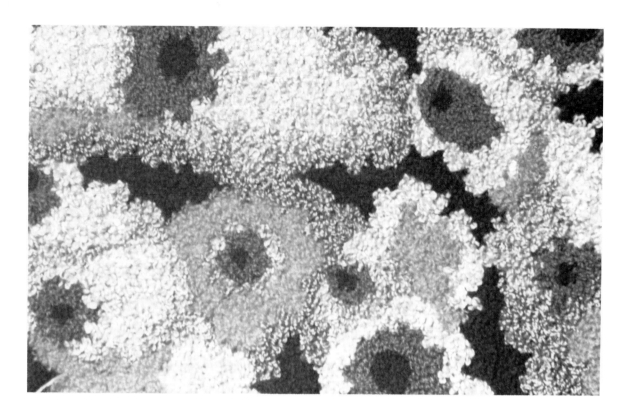

be set between 6 and 7 o'clock. (Diagram 16). Position the machine facing the front and turn the needle to face the back of machine; remove the pressure foot rubber and work with the claw foot. The above adjustments will give a continuous loop stitch.

Hand Movement

The hand movement of the crank handle must be in complete rounds all the time, to produce interlocking circles throughout the work. (Diagram 17). This is to hold the work secure in the fabric. However, if a light or single line is required, it should be held in place by a free running stitch on a fine fabric. (Running stitch worked on the Irish or Domestic machines). On a heavy fabric an iron-on staflex could be used as backing to secure the work. These last two suggestions will of course depend on the application of the moss stitch. If it is for a garment it must be secure for wearing and cleaning. There are many uses for the moss stitch in which the security of the stitch must be given consideration. Different threads can be used for moss stitch as for the chain stitch; the needle and nipple size will vary with the thickness of the thread being used. To achieve a high loop set the needle in a high position, with a loose underneath tension and a short stitch length. For a short loop set the needle to medium position, with a medium underneath tension and a short stitch length.

Figure 7 Moss stitch has a raised pile – loop stitch

Diagram 16 Shuttle position set between six and seven o'clock

Diagram 17 Hand movement to produce the interlocking circles

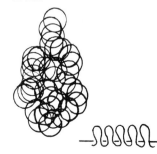

Table II Moss stitch variation

Stitch	Needle size		Nipple size	Thread size	Tension	Needle height	Length
	new	*old*					
small	90	3	3	50 thread	medium	medium to high	short
	100	4	4	metal thread	medium to loose	medium to high	medium to short
medium	110	5	5	floss	loose	high	medium to short
large	120	6	6	2-ply wool	loose	high	short
	130	7	7	perlé	loose	high	short
	140	8	8				

There is no need to fasten off moss stitch, just cut the top of the last loop that has been worked.

6. Cord or Two Cord

The appearance of this stitch is that of its title, a cord. There is one thread used for the chain stitch and a second thread or threads used for the surface. The surface thread is wound around each chain stitch made by the machine, therefore it is the chain stitch which holds the cord in place on the surface of the fabric. Various surface threads can be used to produce a wide variety of cords. (Diagram 8). Use soft threads as these work much better; stiff threads are very difficult to use or to achieve a smooth cord. (Refer to Table III, p. 38).

Figure 8 Cord or two cord. Cord worked on a knitted fabric using one end of chenille or one end of variegated wool or two ends of 2-ply wool on the carrier bobbin

The Cog for Cord

To enable the L3 Cornely to work a cord stitch, the machine must have the single cog connected to revolve the barrel. The barrel is the larger section above the stem holding the nipple. Directly above the barrel is a straight cog with a small cog to the right. At the right of these should be the single cog that revolves the barrel and this cog is used to adjust the barrel position. (Diagram 18).

Adjustment

For the adjustment, release the screw directly above the right hand cog; this cog will drop down to show the flat sided cog rod. (Diagram 19). The barrel is quite free for any adjustment to be made. Push the cog up, interlocking the teeth section with the small cog, while making sure the screw is to the flat side of the rod. Tighten the screw to secure the cog and barrel in the correct position.

Diagram 19 Adjust the barrel position by the release of the single cog

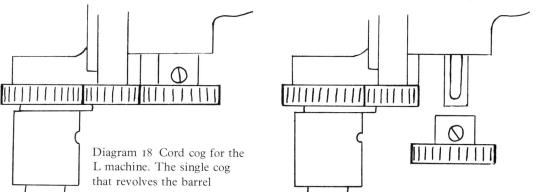

Diagram 18 Cord cog for the L machine. The single cog that revolves the barrel

The LG3 Cornely should also have the straight cog as above; in addition it has the front plate for easier adjustment. The front plunger is pulled out to neutral. Then adjust the barrel and hold in the new position with the left hand while putting the plunger into the hole marked '1'. (Figure 9). Turn the top wheel backwards to ensure that the machine has stopped after one complete stitch and not at a half stitch, then check the attachment position.

Figure 9 The LG3 front plate. For easier adjustment the plunger is set into the hole marked '1'

Figure 10 (a) Cord attachments. Shown (from left to right) in the top line are the carrier tension screw, the carrier screw and the carrier. In the bottom line is the A guide thumb screw, older and newer types of carrier and A guide, and a carrier bobbin

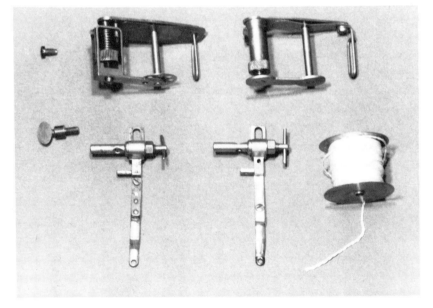

Chain Stitch

The chain stitch should be fairly small and tight, using a small needle and nipple. In stating this, however, the chain stitch must be able to accommodate the surface threads that are being used. Always try a sample of the chain stitch first and check it will be adequate in length to accommodate the surface threads; also check that the needle is not too low for these threads to pass underneath the needle with ease.

Cord Attachments

The attachments used are the carrier, which holds the bobbin, and the A guide, which supports the surface threads from the carrier bobbin to the lower position inside the pressure foot. (Figure 10a).

Carrier and A guide

To identify the sections of the carrier from right to left: the metal loop is the thread guide; the straight rod is the bobbin holder; the tension screw is at the lower end of the spring, which is surrounded by metal supports with shoulders at the top; and the flat fixing plate has the screw hole in the centre of two small holes. The carrier is attached to the revolving barrel of the machine with the carrier screw.

To do this easily, locate the carrier position on the barrel. There is only one place for this; it has two protruding pins with a centre screw hole. (Diagram 20). Hold the carrier in the left hand, place the screw in the centre hole of the flat fixing plate, place this in position and secure the screw with a screwdriver in the right hand.

The A guide is held in position with the thumb screw; there is only one place for this on the revolving barrel and that is marked 'A'. Place the lower section of the A guide inside the round pressure foot, with the left

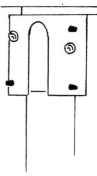

Diagram 20 Corner position of the barrel

Figure 10 (b) Cord attachments fitted. (The cord cog can be seen at the top right of the photo.) The carrier must be on the left with the A guide on the right

33

hand, and turn the thumb screw with the right hand. Face the machine to the front; make sure the stitch has been completed and check the attachment positions. The carrier must be on the left with the A guide on the right; if necessary, re-position by adjustment to the cog for the cord. (Figure 10b).

Winding the Bobbin

Winding the multiple ends for the bobbin is similar to winding the spool for chain. Use the wheel spike and thread holder, with three spools of the same colour thread. Place these on the thread holder with the thread coming alternately from the spools, top, under, top; this way they will not tangle. (Figure 11). Wind the three threads onto one spool. Having wound sufficient thread onto the spool place this onto the thread holder, one top, one under, one top; this will make six ends that can be wound

Figure 11 The thread coming alternately from the spools. From left to right they are top, under, top

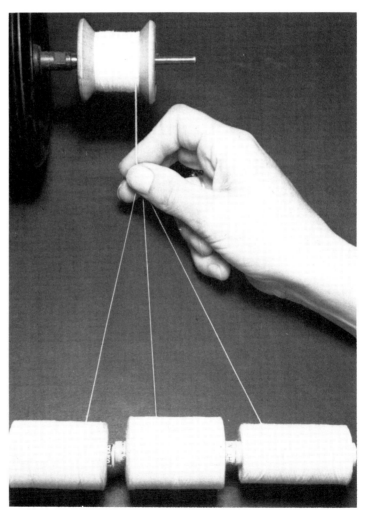

onto the bobbin. It is very important that the bobbin should be wound smoothly and evenly; the thread must never protrude above the sides of the bobbin. Re-wind the ends onto another bobbin if they are uneven.

Threading the Attachment

To thread the carrier and A guide have the required number of threads wound smoothly onto the carrier bobbin. The number of threads used will depend on the size of cord to be produced.

Place the left thumb on the shoulders of the carrier, push straight down and swing the lower section bobbin support out with the forefinger. (Figure 12). Push the bobbin upward onto the rod with the thread coming

Figure 12 Place the left thumb on the shoulders of the carrier, push straight down and swing the lower section bobbin support out with the forefinger, until there is enough space for the bobbin to be put onto the rod

to the outside and swing the lower section back to hold the bobbin in position. The bobbin rod must fit inside the centre hole of the lower section to achieve the tension adjustments that will be required. Take the bobbin threads through the loop of the thread guide on the carrier, then through the top, centre and lower thread holes of the A guide. Thread the lower A guide hole from the outside to the inside; the threads must be drawn out underneath the pressure foot. Take these surface threads across the front of the nipple as the pressure foot is lowered on the fabric to start work. (Figure 13a).

Figure 13b shows how the barrel turns the carrier and the A guide to complete one full stitch.

Carrier Tension

The carrier tension needs adjustment throughout the use of the cord stitch. At the beginning of the work the bobbin would be wound almost full but never above the edges of the bobbin. When the bobbin is full the carrier tension would need to be fairly tight; as the threads are used from the bobbin the carrier tension needs loosening to retain the same thickness cord throughout the work. Once the chain stitch adjustments have been set for a small tight stitch these can be left throughout the work.

Figure 13 (a) Thread the carrier and A guide, take the surface threads across the front of the nipple

Adjustment

To loosen the carrier tension turn the screw clockwise or away from the bobbin outwards (the reverse to tighten it). Always try a sample stitch on a small piece of fabric before the final piece of work is put under the pressure foot.

If the tension is too loose and there is no more adjustment on the carrier tension screw, check that the bobbin rod is in the centre hole of the lower section bobbin support. A little more tension can be achieved by turning the top thread holder of the A guide. Turn the top outwards and this will make the thread loop round the top thread holder and tighten the thread flow.

Finishing the Cord

The last chain stitch must be caught in the same way as when working chain stitch. Loosen the underneath thread by pulling it forward, hold the work firm while raising the pressure foot, put the hook knife between the machine table and the underneath of the work, pull the chain thread forward and cut it. Loosen the threads from the carrier, turning the bobbin by hand, and carefully take the work out from under the pressure

Figure 13 (b) The barrel turns the carrier and A guide round, to complete one full stitch

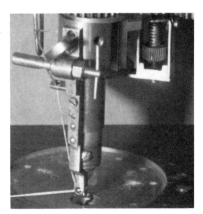

foot. Make sure the chain stitch has been caught and cut the top threads. Take all the ends of thread to the underneath of the work, sew these to the back of the chain stitch with a few oversew stitches and cut away the ends of thread, leaving 1.5cm ($\frac{5}{8}$in) at the back of the work. If a join is made in the cord it should look continuous; the cord should not be made to overlap at a joint but should butt end to end. The ends of thread are then crossed over the cord (Figure 13c) and taken to the back either side of the cord line. Overstitch the thread on the back of the work as before.

Figure 13 (c) Join the cord. Take the ends of thread to the back of the work by the sides of the cord

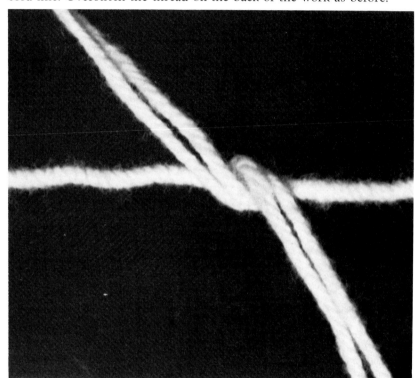

Table III   Cord stitch variation

Stitch	Needle size		Nipple size	Chain thread	Bobbin threads
	new	old			
fine	90	3	3	50 thread	thread five ends
	90	3	3	50 thread	metal thread two or three ends
medium	90	3	3	50 thread	cotton eight ends
	90	3	3	40 thread	wool 2-ply two ends
	90	3	3	40 thread	metal thread four ends
large	100	4	4	36 thread	wool 2-ply three ends
	100	4	4	36 thread	chenille one end

7. Retard

The appearance of this stitch is a floating thread or threads over the chosen number of chain stitches. One thread is used for the chain stitch and the surface thread from the carrier makes the floating thread. For the 1 to 3 retard the surface thread is under every third stitch and floats over the stitches in between. (Figure 14).

The Cogs for Retard

The L3 Cornely machine must have the cord cog taken off and replaced by the retard cogs. The reason for this is to retard the revolutions of the barrel to each complete chain stitch. (This stitch could be simulated by using the cord cog. Have a very long chain stitch length with a very loose

Figure 14 Retard one to three stitch. This was worked with a fine metal thread chain and three ends of floss on the bobbin

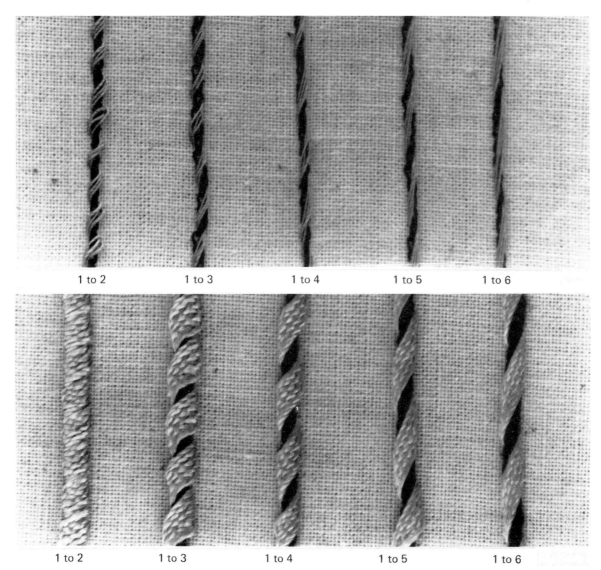

| 1 to 2 | 1 to 3 | 1 to 4 | 1 to 5 | 1 to 6 |

| 1 to 2 | 1 to 3 | 1 to 4 | 1 to 5 | 1 to 6 |

Top:

Figure 15 (a) Cotton retard. The number of retard revolutions of the barrel to each complete chain stitch

Figure 15 (b) Braid retard

carrier tension). The most used retard is the 1 to 3, one revolution of the barrel to three chain stitches. (Figures 15a and b).

Take the cord cog off the machine and fit the multiple retard cogs in its place. (Diagram 21). For the 1 to 3 retard the multiple three-cog top section has a flat plate with a centre hole. This is fitted to the lower back section of the machine support, interlocking the teeth with the front small cog; screw in securely. The small retard cog is fitted onto the flat sided rod with the teeth section to the top. Interlock the teeth with the back cog and the screw to the flat side of the rod; screw in securely.

The LG3 machine has the front plate with the different number positions for retard. (Figure 16). The plunger must be set securely in the numbered hole; this can be from 2 to 6 and the same retardation of the barrel will come into action as with the L3 machine and the retard cogs.

40

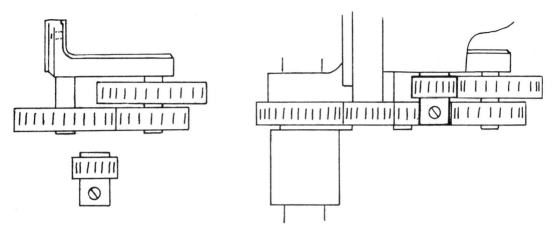

Therefore, if hole 5 is selected the revolution of the barrel will be one to every five stitches. Pull the plunger straight outwards, turn right into rest position, select number required. As this plunger is moved directly over the hole, the interlocking of cogs inside the machine will be felt with the movement. This is an easy hand movement – no tools are needed. Release the plunger from the rest position and make sure the inside pin is right in the selected hole, not resting on the front plate.

The 2 to 6 retard variation can be worked on the L3 machine; to be able to do this the retard cogs must be changed for each retardation.

Diagram 21 Retard attachments for the flat plate section on the L3/LG3 machine. The 1 to 3 multiple cogs for the retard stitch (left), and the retard cogs fitted in place (right)

Figure 16 Front plate of the LG3 machine. The plunger must be set secure in the numbered hole

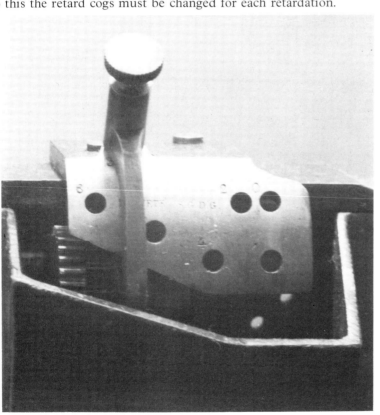

Chain Stitch

The chain stitch should be the same as for cord. However, there are many variations that can be used for retard. If a thicker thread or wool is required for a variation make sure the needle and nipple size will accommodate the chain stitch thread. (Refer to Table IV, p. 43).

Retard Attachments

Carrier and A guide

These are the same as for cord; the carrier and the A guide are fitted in the same positions.

Threading the Attachments

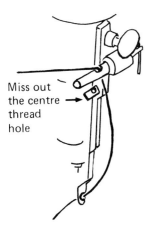

Miss out the centre thread hole →

Threading the carrier is the same as for cord, but threading the A guide is slightly different. Go through the top hole and straight down to the lower one, missing out the centre hole. (Diagram 22). If using a slub thread make sure the slub section will pass easily through the lower hole; the thread could be looped over the thumb screw and then must be threaded through the lower hole, always from the outside to the inside, then underneath the pressure foot.

Diagram 22 Thread the A guide for retard

Carrier Tension

It will be found when working that a fairly loose carrier tension will be needed for retard. If the tension is too tight the result will be a straight floating thread and even a slight gathering of the fabric, as well as pulling the chain stitch over the carrier thread. The gathering of the fabric would also be the result if the stitch length was too long, with a tight chain tension and a tight carrier tension.

Finishing the Retard

Finish the ends off and join as for cord. To make the retard look continuous oversew the ends on the wrong side of the work.

Table IV   Retard stitch variation

Stitch	Needle size		Nipple size	Chain thread	Bobbin threads
	new	*old*			
fine	90	3	3	50 thread	three ends
	90	3	3	metal thread	metal thread two ends
medium	90	3	3	50 thread	floss three ends
	100	4	4	rayon twist	rayon twist five ends
	100	4	4	metal thread	wool 2-ply one or two ends
large	90	3	3	40 thread	five ends
	120	6	6	wool	wool 2-ply three ends
	90	3	3	40 thread	fine ribbon one end

8. Three Cord

The appearance of three cord is similar to the two cord; however, as a third thread is used for a padding the three cord is more round in appearance. The two cord is slightly flat as there is no padding to support the cord. For the three cord variation refer to Table V, p. 47.

Figure 17 Three cord. The padding used in this stitch will support the background vertical lines. This design was traced onto vanishing muslin only, then a chain stitch mesh was worked covering the solid areas. The three cord straight vertical lines were worked over the chain and then the solid areas of cord were worked last. As different thicknesses of cotton were used for the cord the bobbin had two, three and four threads wound on, with two and four threads used for the pad threads

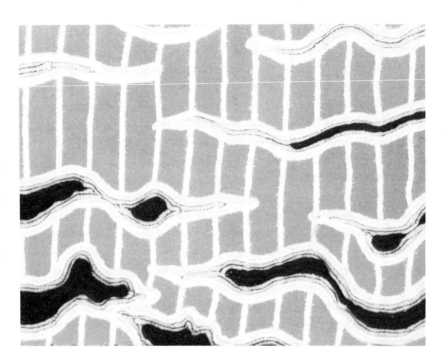

Needle Bar

For the L3 and LG3 Cornely working three cord, the hook front of the needle must be screwed in to face the front of the needle bar. (Figure 18). The front of the needle bar is the hollow section, the back is round and solid. Place the needle bar back in the machine but leave the needle raised.

Stem and Holder

To be able to work three cord the stem and holder must be fitted for the third or top thread which is used for the padding. (Figure 19a). Select the size stem for the size cord that is to be worked; the sizes are from small to large: 1, 1.25, 1.50, 1.75, 2, 2.25, 2.50, 2.75, 3, 3.25. Remove the pressure

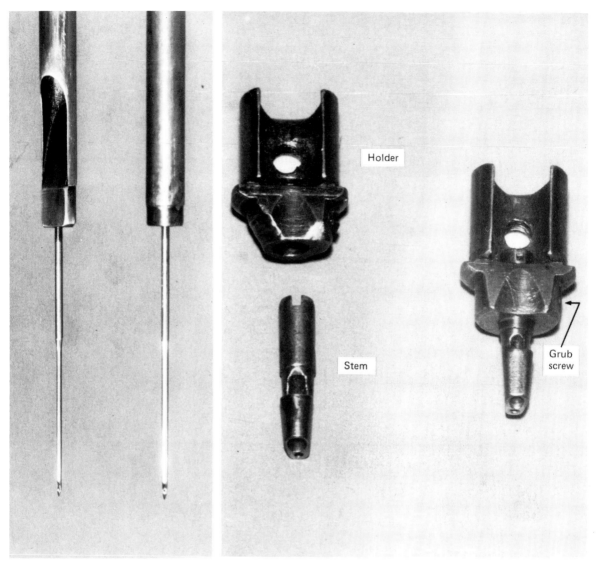

Holder

Stem

Grub screw

foot and round needle plate as before. The nipple and holder must be removed; to do this remove the front screw immediately above the nipple and pull nipple and holder downwards to remove.

Push the stem holder into the main stem of the machine, with the cut-away section facing front. Screw in position with the screw previously removed, but this must now be screwed in at the back. Turn the crank handle to the back for easier access. Turn the crank handle to the front; at the right side of the stem holder locate the small grub screw and release this, but never take it right out. Push the stem up into the holder with the hole section facing front, and tighten the grub screw to secure. Replace the round needle plate, replace the pressure foot and lower the needle into working position. Work a sample of the chain stitch; this should be adjusted to work a tight chain stitch as for two cord.

Above, left
Figure 18 Needle bar. (Left) The front of the needle bar with the hook needle facing the front. (Right) The back of the needle bar with the hook needle facing the back

Figure 19 (a) (Left) Holder and stem facing the front. (Right) Holder and stem fitted together

Attachments

The carrier and A guide are fitted as for two cord; the threading and tensions are also the same as those used for two cord. (Figure 19b).

Top Threading and Tension

This is the third thread used for three cord. Again the thread is wound onto a spool with shoulders, the same as that used for the underneath of the machine when working chain. The spool is placed on the top spool holder which is located on the top arm section of the machine, with the thread coming over the top. (Figure 20). This has a tension adjustment; the lever is easily visible at the back. For a loose tension push the lever left towards the needle bar, for a tight tension right towards top wheel. Push the ladder in a vertical position ready to support the top thread.

Below, left
Figure 19 (b) The holder and stem fitted into the main stem of the machine

Below, right
Figure 20 Spool placed on the top spool holder

Carrier

Cord cog

← A guide

Holder and stem

Tension adjustment

↑ Ladder in a vertical position

↑ Top spool holder

This top thread must go down through the needle bar and the stem. For this, use the small link brass chain with a loop of strong thread at one end. Pass the top thread through the chain thread to make a second loop of 20cm (8in) and pass the chain down the needle bar while holding the second loop firm in the right hand. When the chain comes through the holder at the bottom pull it forward with the left hand while feeding the top thread through. Take the chain out to reveal the top thread; this must then be threaded through the stem underneath the round pressure foot. Bring the carrier threads and top threads across the front of the stem before working.

Finishing the Three Cord

Finish the ends off as for two cord; the joining is also the same. To make the three cord look continuous oversew the ends on the wrong side of the work.

Table V   Three cord variation

Stitch	Needle size		Stem size	Chain thread	Bobbin threads	Top thread
	new	*old*				
fine	90	3	1.25	50 thread	thread five ends	thread three ends
	90	3	1.75	50 thread	wool 2-ply two ends	wool 2-ply one end
medium	90	3	2	50 thread	thread eight ends	thread five ends
	90	3	2.50	50–40 thread	wool 2-ply three ends	wool 2-ply two ends
	90	3	2.50	50 thread	floss six ends	floss four ends
large	90	3	3	40 thread	wool 4-ply two ends	wool 4-ply one end

Metal thread can easily be used for three cord. The number of ends used will depend on the thickness of the thread and the thickness of cord required.

9. Pad Stitch

This is the same for the L3 and LG3 machines. The pad stitch appearance is the same as three cord. A different stem is used – the one piece stem and holder unit. It is possible to produce a heavier stitch similar to that of a three cord by using the larger size pad stem (Figure 21a), and to simulate what is known as Boulogne stitch, using only the pad thread, which should be quite thick or a fine ribbon. (Figure 21b). The stem number sizes are: 1.50, 1.75, 2, 2.25, 2.50, 2.75, from small to large. The hole for the pad thread is set to the back, of the machine with the needle to the front. For the pad stitch variations refer to Table VI, p. 50.

Figure 21 (a) Pad stitch will produce a very thick cord stitch. For the above stitch one end of chunky knitting wool was wound onto the bobbin with one end of thick cotton used for the pad

Figure 21 (b) Boulogne stitch. A thick wool was used coming from the top of the machine and through the pad stem, make a small curl over the wool each side

Needle Bar

For the L3 and LG3 working pad stitch the front hook of the needle must face the solid back of the needle bar. Remove the needle bar as before and turn the hook of the needle to face the solid round back of the needle bar. (Figure 18). Place the needle bar in the machine but leave it raised.

Pad Stem

Remove the stem and holder, if in the machine, or nipple and holder, as described before, with the pressure foot and plate removed. Select the size of pad stem needed for the thickness of stitch required. Test the pad thread through the stem before fitting. (Figure 21c). The pad stem and holder is pushed into the main stem of the machine, with the large pad

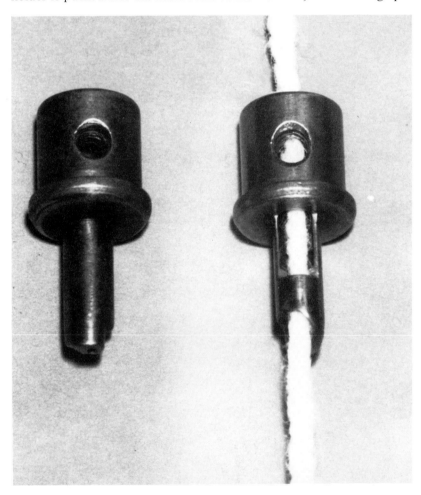

Figure 21 (c) Pad stem. (Left) Pad stem: the front. (Right) Pad stem: the back with the padding thread

hole to the back and the small needle hole to the front. Screw the pad stem in position with the screw previously removed, but this must now be screwed in at the front of machine, the same as the nipple and holder. Replace the round needle plate and the pressure foot; lower the needle into working position. The stitch should be adjusted to work a tight chain as for two and three cord; however, remember it must accommodate the carrier threads that are being used.

Attachment

The carrier and A guide are fitted as before and threaded as for two and three cord.

Top Threads

This is the same threading as for three cord method, using the top reel holder and the small brass chain. (Figure 20). However, for this stitch the pad thread will now be to the back of needle, not to the front of the needle as with three cord.

Finishing Off Ends

This is the same as for two and three cord, and the joining must be very accurate.

Table VI Pad stitch variation

Stitch	Needle size		Stem size	Chain thread	Bobbin threads	Top threads
	new	*old*				
fine	90	3	1.50	50 thread	rayon twist five ends	rayon twist four ends
	90	3	1.75	50 thread	wool 2-ply three ends	wool 2-ply two ends
medium	90	3	2	50 thread	floss six ends	floss four ends
	90	3	2.25	40 thread	metal thread six ends	metal thread four ends
large	90	3	2.50	50 thread	fine ribbon one end	cotton six ends
	90	3	2.75	40 thread	wool 4-ply two ends	wool 4-ply two ends

Boulogne Stitch

This stitch has the appearance of retard stitch with the floating thread over the chain stitches. However, the floating thread is not taken under the chain stitch by the A guide, but is held in place by working a small curl movement with the underneath handle. In fact it can be worked as the retard stitch with the one revolution to six stitches and a fine ribbon or thick wool on the carrier. If working this way great care must be taken if the design requires a lot of turning. The turn should be made as the carrier thread is caught by the sixth stitch, otherwise this thread will loop to the shortest distance, thus revealing the chain stitch making the turn.

Using the pad stem only for this stitch, do not use the carrier or A guide; have a fine ribbon or a thick wool for the top thread. It is the way the machine is controlled that can give a good appearance to this stitch. The top thread must be caught down with the chain stitch, therefore a very small curl must be made to work over the top thread. The length of the floating thread will depend on how frequently the curl is made. This can be used for a solid filling or a straight line design. (Figure 21b).

10. Stitch Problems

Personal awareness and observation comes very much to the fore when setting the Cornely to work all the different stitches. If the cord, three cord or pad stitch do not produce a satisfactory result, then more adjustments must be made to the machine. Examine the stitch sample that has been worked and analyse what is wrong. If the following visual mistakes occur the suggested adjustments will help to correct the stitches.

Stitch Length

If the threads from the carrier show a definite division as they wrap the chain stitch (Figure 22a), this shows the stitch length is too long for the

amount of threads wound on the carrier. There are two ways to overcome this problem and produce a smooth stitch:
1. Shorten the stitch length to accommodate the carrier threads.
2. Add more threads to the carrier and fill in the division.

Needle Position and Underneath Tension

If the chain stitch shows through the cord or on a curve, or at a corner (Figure 22b), there are two ways to overcome this problem:
1. First make sure the needle has not moved up; this can happen if the needle bar thumb screw is not tight. The needle could be too high; therefore lower the needle position.
2. The underneath chain tension could be too loose; tighten it.

Top Thread Tension

If the cord is being pulled away from the chain stitch on a curve or corner, producing a slip stitch (Figure 22c), then the top tension is too tight. Loosen the tension on the top spool until the cord is resting on the chain stitch. Do not make this too loose – if it is, the thread will show through the side of the cord in loops.

Carrier Tension

If the carrier tension is too loose the result will be an uneven cord; if it is too tight a very thin cord will be produced; also the carrier threads may tend to be cut and the machine will become too stiff to use. (Figure 23).

Slub Thread

A slub thread can be used to produce a cord. It is important to make sure the holes in the A guide are large enough to receive the slubs. If there is any tightness as the slubs reach the holes, it will pull the cord away from the surface of the fabric. The centre hole in the A guide may be omitted, provided the floating thread is not too loose for it to be caught up in the revolving action while working. Avoid a tight tension on the carrier as this will impede the smooth flow of the thread.

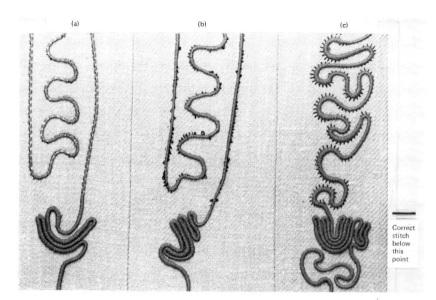

(a)   (b)   (c)

Correct
stitch
below
this
point

Figure 22 Stitch length

Figure 23 Carrier tension

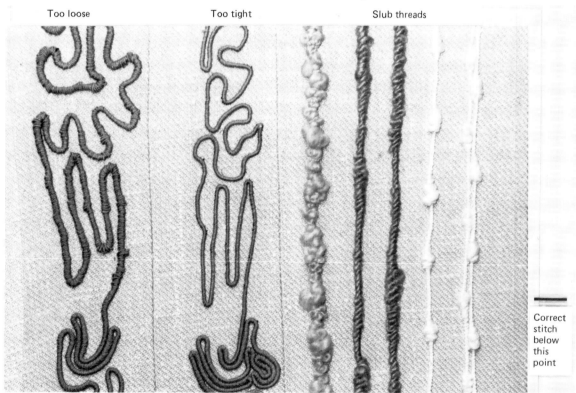

Too loose   Too tight   Slub threads

Correct
stitch
below
this
point

11. Ribbon

This is the same for the L3 and LG3 machines. The size of ribbon used will depend on the size of the ribbon stem. The ribbon must fit the stem exactly. This is held in position by the chain stitch through the centre of the ribbon. It will depend on how this is worked as to the result; if straight lines are worked the ribbon will be flat, if curls or a close wave direction then the edge of the ribbon will stand up. (Figure 24).

Figure 24 Ribbon stitched with a metal thread showing how the ribbon will curl up when sewn with a movement

Needle Bar

Using the L3 and LG3 machine for ribbon, the front hook of the needle must face the hollow front side of the needle bar, the same as for three cord.

Ribbon Stem

The ribbon stem has a fairly flat horizontal section on the flat side of the vertical stem. (Figure 25). Before placing the stem in the machine check that the ribbon will fit the horizontal section of the ribbon stem exactly. If the stem is too big the ribbon will move about and slip from underneath the chain stitch, instead of the chain being in the centre of the ribbon.

Place the stem holder in the machine as for three cord and screw the ribbon stem in position with the flat section facing directly front. The

54

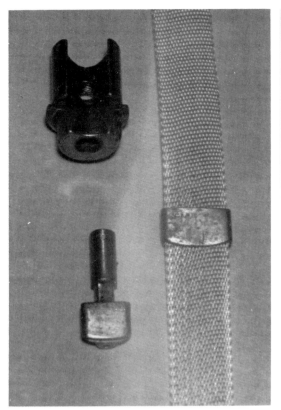

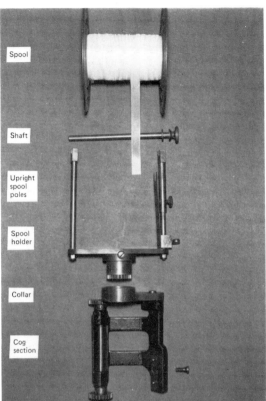

Spool

Shaft

Upright spool poles

Spool holder

Collar

Cog section

chain stitch should be medium with a fairly round chain stitch, not a loose or looped chain stitch.

Top Attachments

The top attachment supports the ribbon spool directly over the top of the needle bar. The attachments are in two sections, the cog section with the collar and the top spool holder. (Figure 26a). Hold the cog section with the cogs to the left, the collar to the top and the flat section to the right. On the lower flat section there are two pins; in the centre of these is the screw hole forming the fixing plate. This fixing plate is fitted to the top back of the machine support. Place the collar over the needle bar and locate the fixing position with the fixing plate while interlocking the lower cog of the attachment into the top cog of the machine. Screw the fixing plate in securely; to make this easier lean over the top of the machine. Turn the handle of the machine to face directly front, then place the cog of the spool holder section into the collar. Again interlock the two cogs. The spool holder must have the two upright spool holder poles on the left and the adjustable tension and pole on the right. This will then hold the spool on the spool shaft in line with the ribbon stem for the easy straight flow of the ribbon. (Figure 26b).

Above, left
Figure 25 At the top left of the photo is the holder as used for three cord, and below it is a ribbon stem. As shown on the right, the ribbon must fit the stem width exactly

Figure 26 (a) Ribbon attachments

55

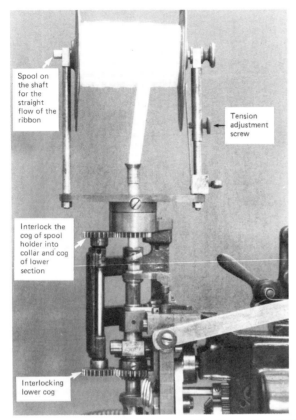

Spool on the shaft for the straight flow of the ribbon

Tension adjustment screw

Interlock the cog of spool holder into collar and cog of lower section

Interlocking lower cog

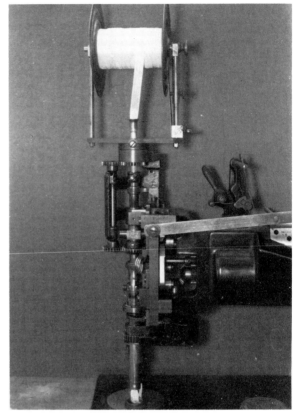

Figure 26 (b) Ribbon attachments in position

Above, right
Figure 26 (c) Ribbon threading, showing the straight flow of the ribbon

Winding the Ribbon

When winding the ribbon onto the spool it must be wound on flat and evenly; if the ribbon is twisted it will work through the needle bar and crease as it is pulled through the stem.

Threading the Top

The spool is placed in position on the spool shaft supported by the poles, with the ribbon coming from the top to the front of the machine. This is kept flat while passing through the loop of the small link brass chain and down the needle bar. Keep the ribbon flat without any twist. Cut this diagonally and pass it through the stem, pushing it under the needle to the back of machine. (Figure 26c).

Top Tension

The adjustable tension is by the right-hand upright pole. For the adjustment locate the round solid screw near the lower section of this pole. Turn the screw clockwise onto the tension lever to tighten the tension on the top spool; this will be pushed at the top onto the spool. Reverse the screw anti-clockwise to loosen the tension. If this is not loose enough use a length of thread to tie the top of the tension lever to the top of the pole.

If using the new top attachment the tension is adjustable by moving the spool holder rod. The rod has a flip-down catch at one end to hold the spool in position. Move the catch down with the spool in place on the rod; release the solid top screw to push or pull the rod through the spool. The closer the spool is pushed onto the tension lever the tighter the tension.

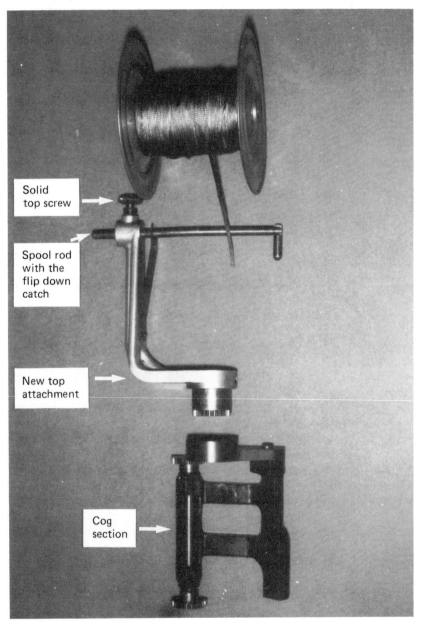

Figure 27 New braid attachments

Solid top screw

Spool rod with the flip down catch

New top attachment

Cog section

The further away the spool is from the tension lever the looser the tension. Always make sure the adjustable solid screw is tight down on the rod before working the machine. (Figure 27).

Underneath Thread

Cotton or a metal thread can be used for the chain stitch; both should be workable with a 90 needle. If the stem has not been drilled to take a larger needle, a thicker thread cannot be used.

Finishing Off the Ends

The ribbon and chain end are taken through to the back of the work with a large needle. Sew to the back of the chain stitches by oversewing; cut the ribbons off, leaving not more than 2cm ($\frac{3}{4}$in). If there is a join within the work, make it as inconspicuous as possible when taking it through to the back.

12. Braid

This is the same for the L3 and LG3 machine. In order to produce braid the same top attachments are used as for ribbon. This stitch requires the use of the shoe, spring and flat faced stem (Figure 28) instead of the ribbon stem or the three cord stem. The braid is normally stitched through the centre with the chain stitch. There are different size shoes for the different thicknesses of braids, and this is also a most successful way of using mohair wool with a fine shoe. (Figure 29). There are shoes for stitching edge braid and edge stitched cord; however, the braid and cord must fit exactly, otherwise this can prove to be very troublesome. The braid and cord can quite easily slip out from underneath the needle, the

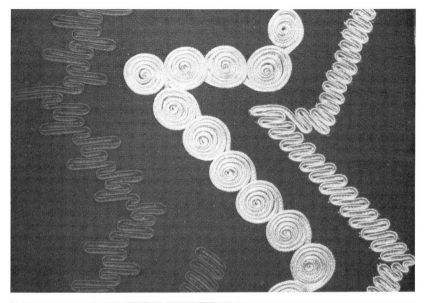

Figure 28 Braid stitch using a Russia and Lacet braid

Figure 29 Mohair wool stitched with a metal thread

result being that the braid and cord will not be stitched at all. The shoe sizes are from small to large: 1.50, 1.75, 2, 2.25, 2.50, 2.75, 3, 3.25, 3.50, to very large 4.50.

Needle Bar

For the L3 and LG3 machine working braid, the front hook of the needle must face the hollow front side of the needle bar, the same as for three cord. Place the needle bar back in the machine but leave it raised.

Stem Spring and Shoe

Remove the pressure foot, round plate and whichever stem is fitted in the machine. Try the braid through the hole in the shoe; this should be an exact fit. The shoe should never be too large; if it is the braid will not be stitched through the centre. Have the three cord holder fitted in the machine stem with the holding screw to the back.

Place the flat faced stem through the centre of the spring and into the shoe; twist the spring so that the lower end of spring is underneath the top lip of the shoe to hold the shoe in place while working. (Figure 30a). Push the top section of the stem inside the holder, with the flat face of the stem and protruding part of the shoe facing the front; hold this upwards. Slip the round plate underneath so that the spring and shoe will not get lodged inside the shuttle. Release the spring and shoe, push the stem upwards as

Figure 30 (a) Shoe spring and flat-faced stem

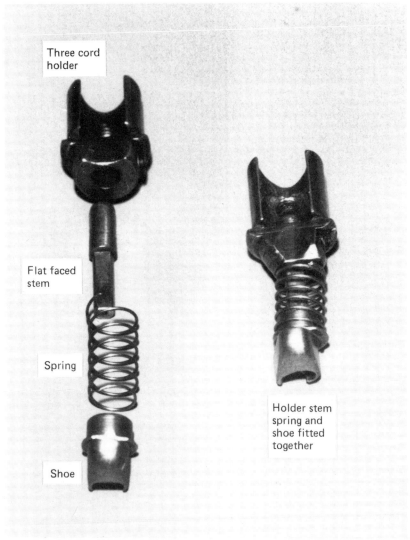

Three cord holder

Flat faced stem

Spring

Shoe

Holder stem spring and shoe fitted together

Spring
end under
top lip of
the shoe

far as it will go and make sure the shoe is facing the front. Secure the stem in place with the grub screw at the right-hand side of the holder. It will be seen now that the spring keeps the shoe right down, resting on the round plate. (Figure 30b).

This is an aid to guide the braid right onto the surface of the fabric, therefore the shoe must be raised by hand every time to see the needle, to thread the braid and to put the fabric underneath. Position the round plate with the needle in a centre hole position; secure in place with the solid screw. Replace the pressure foot and secure in position. Set the needle at medium height or sufficiently high to allow the braid to pass underneath. Try the chain stitch with cotton or metal thread (whichever is to be used on the braid) to establish a good stitch.

Figure 30 (b) Stem spring and shoe in position with the braid hole in the shoe facing the front of machine and resting on the round plate

Winding Braid and Threading Top

Wind the braid onto the top spool; this must be kept flat, with no twist, and must be even. The braid is passed through the needle bar, keeping it flat, as for ribbon. Then thread the shoe, cut the braid diagonally and push from the front to the back, passing underneath the needle.

Top Tension

If the braid is dragging, adjust the top tension to loosen it a little; if the braid is coming through too loose, tighten the top tension.

Finishing Off the Ends

Take through as for ribbon, sewing braid to the back of the chain stitch.

13. Whip Stitch

This is the same for the L3 and LG3 machine. There are three other names for this stitch: Gimp, Paris or French stitch. The appearance of the stitch is that of spikes forming the outer circle, to a fine cord forming the small inner circle. This is formed by the co-ordination of the hand movement to work continuous circles or curls. If worked in a straight line the appearance is that of a fine cord with loops either side, the latter being formed by the chain stitch. (Figure 31).

There are three ways of achieving this stitch:

1. Using the gimp fitting with the stem spring and shoe.
2. Using the gimp fitting with the three cord stem and holder.
3. Using the gimp carrier A guide and small pad stem.

Needle Bar

For the L3 and LG3 working whip stitch the front hook of the needle must face the solid back of the needle bar. This is the same as for pad stitch; the top thread must be allowed to pass to the back of machine. Place the needle bar back in the machine but leave it raised.

Figure 31 Whip stitch
worked on leather using a
perlé thread on the carrier
and through the needle bar,
with a cotton thread
underneath

Figure 32 (a) Whip stitch
attachments

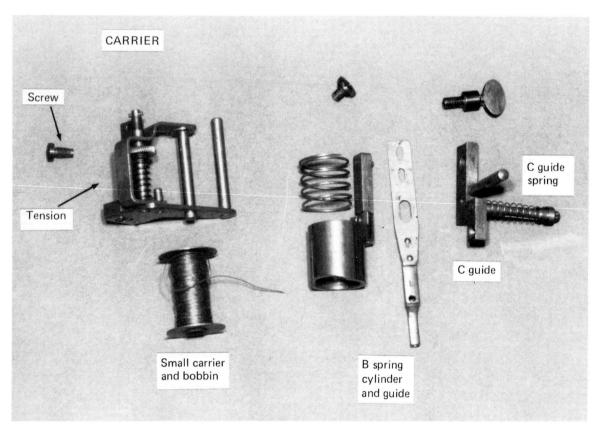

CARRIER

Screw

Tension

C guide
spring

C guide

Small carrier
and bobbin

B spring
cylinder
and guide

1. Attachments or Gimp Fittings

These are: small carrier, B cylinder, spring, C guide, stem, spring and small shoe. (Figure 32a). Use the gimp fittings on the machine as for method 1 above, together with the tension adjustments and working movement. Remove the pressure foot, round plate and whichever stem is in the machine. Have the machine facing front; place the spring and B cylinder on the main tube of the machine, pushing the upright lever into the cut-out position in the barrel. Hold this up firmly while putting the stem holder in the machine, with the opening to the back; secure with the screw at the front of the machine. (Diagram 23). Release B cylinder; it will be held in position by the stem holder screw. Put the stem spring and shoe in the holder, with the shoe facing the back of the machine; secure with the grub screw.

Position the round plate with the needle in a centre hole position; secure this in place with the solid screw. Replace the pressure foot and secure it in position. Screw the small carrier in position with the carrier screw; this is the same position as for the cord carrier. Secure the C guide in the C position on the barrel with the thumb screw. Secure the B guide with the special short screw; put the lower part inside the pressure foot, which is adjustable for low, medium and high position, as with the cord A guide. Lower the needle into a high working position. The stitch should be fairly loose; try this to make sure there is no slipping.

Diagram 23 Attachments or
gimp fittings

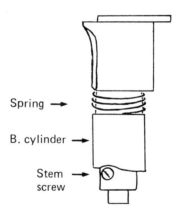

Spring ➡

B. cylinder ➡

Stem ➡
screw

Threading the Attachments

Wind the small bobbin as for the cord bobbin; use a fine but strong thread. Place the bobbin in the carrier, with the thread coming to the outside as for the cord. To open the small carrier pull the top directly upwards until the lower section is above the short pin; swing it outwards as for the cord carrier. Push the bobbin upwards onto the rod, with the thread coming to the outside; swing the top section back to hold the bobbin in position. The bobbin rod must fit inside the hole in the lower

Figure 32 (b) Whip stitch attachments fitted to the machine and threaded for working the stitch

65

Figure 33 To achieve a tight
top tension wind the thread
around the ladder

plate to achieve the tension adjustments that will be required. Take the
thread round the end pin on the carrier then over the top pin of the C
guide. Push the spring back towards the machine stem on the second pin
of the C guide and push the thread from top to bottom through the centre
elongated hole. Thread the lower hole in the C guide from the outside in
towards the machine stem, then take the thread through the top and
bottom holes of the B guide and pass underneath the pressure foot.
(Figure 32b).

Top Thread

This is the third thread and used from the top; it also should be fine but strong. As for the three cord, use the small-link brass chain to take the top thread through the needle bar. Take the thread through the shoe and under the pressure foot. The top tension is the same as for three cord; push the lever forward or left to loosen, back or right to tighten. Push the ladder up into vertical position as whip stitch needs a fairly tight top tension; the thread may have to be wound around the ladder to achieve this. (Figure 33).

Carrier Tension

To tighten the carrier tension turn the screw at the left of the bobbin clockwise or to the left. To loosen, turn the screw anti-clockwise or to the right. Whip stitch needs quite a tight carrier tension to hold the top thread tight in position onto the chain stitch.

Working Whip Stitch

The hand movement of the crank handle must be complete rounds all the time, making fairly large circles that just touch each other. (Diagram 24). As the top and carrier tension are fairly tight, these threads will pull the chain stitch through the fabric to form the claws and so make the small inner circle. Try the stitch first on a piece of fabric to adjust the tensions for a good stitch.

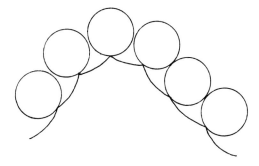

Diagram 24 Hand movement of fairly large circles

2.   Attachments: the Gimp Fitting with the Three Cord Stem and Holder

Use the gimp fittings on the machine as for 1, plus the tension adjustments and working movement. Use a fine three cord stem in the holder facing the back of machine instead of the stem, spring and shoe.

3. Attachments: the Gimp Carrier with the A Guide and Fine Pad Stem

Use the small gimp carrier only plus the cord A guide, instead of the B and C guides. The tension adjustments and working movement are the same as for 1. Use a fine pad stem in the machine as for pad stitch, instead of using the holder stem, spring and shoe.

Finishing Off the Ends

Take ends through as for two and three cord to the back of the work and oversew these ends to the back of the chain stitches.

14.   Care and Maintenance

Care and maintenance of the Cornely is essential for the accurate working of the machine. It will be found that a great deal of cotton and fabric dust will collect in the shuttle. This dust will become compacted and hinder the shuttle movement. Raise the needle, remove the pressure foot and round plate; the dust seen must be removed. Use a broken needle or blunt pin and remove as much as possible; oil the shuttle and work this through until it is clear of any particles. Replace the round plate and pressure foot and bring the needle down.

When using the machine it is important not to let any threads or hair get caught between the cogs. Remove any of these foreign bodies and place a spot of oil on the cogs. Oil the hole directly under the needle bar thumb screw, the moving lever directly left of the stitch length screw, the needle bar support behind this screw and the top foot lever support behind this. Oil the holes along the top arm of the machine and the holes near the top wheel.

Underneath the machine, oil the hole on the crank handle housing and the cogs to the back of the handle. Give the machine a good working through without any cotton. The machine may splash out oil if the

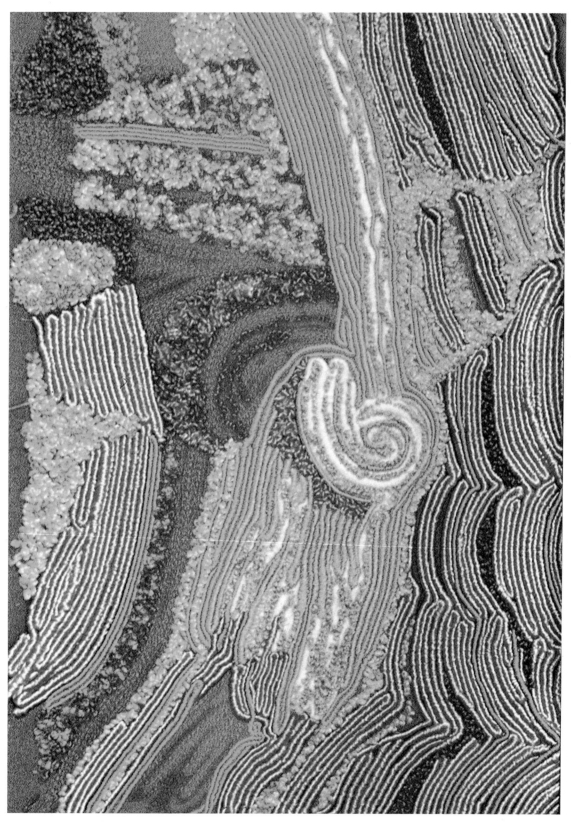

1. The Cornely machine chain, moss and cord stitches have been worked
to produce a varied texture

2. The Irish machine is used here for layer appliqué, satin stitch, open work and the fringe filling texture

application of the oil was heavy; an overall will help stop any soiling of clothes.

Thread the machine for chain stitch and give it a good work through on a piece of waste fabric before starting work again. If working on a light colour fabric after oiling the machine, cover the front and back left-hand side of the machine by pinning a piece of tissue paper around the top section and under the arm section of the machine to help prevent oil marks. (Every care must be taken when using the tissue paper; it should never hinder or get caught in the cog movement of the machine). A dry cleaner may stain some fabric if this has to be used to remove oil marks; try a sample first.

Singer Irish

15. Singer 107W 102 Irish

This machine has one needle which works a lock stitch for straight lines or a zigzag up to 13mm ($\frac{1}{2}$in). (Figure 34). The width of the zigzag is controlled by using the knee bar underneath the machine. It does not have the teeth or feed mechanism with a pressure foot to push the work through at an even length. The fabric is held taut between the two hands or put in a round frame, which is then moved in any direction required. This machine is more frequently used for flat embroidery; however, it can be fitted with attachments for 'Madeira' embroidery.

Figure 34 Singer 107W 102 Irish

When using this machine there is a need for co-ordination and control, which can be achieved with practice and perseverance.

There are many variations of work that can be produced with flat embroidery by using thread, wool or metal thread, different working methods and tension adjustments. The zigzag can be used in its central position to give equal shape either side of the centre, or to give a straight edge with the shape to the right or left side. The easy movement of the knee bar for the control of the width makes this machine very versatile, and when combined with the hand movements gives endless possibilities for interesting machine embroidery.

The fabrics that have been embroidered should always be as flat and smooth as they were before having any stitchery worked on them. This is very important to remember. If any distortion takes place during the stitching it is very difficult, sometimes impossible, to remove. The embroidery can be pressed, but this must always be from the wrong side.

16. The Bobbin

Winding the Bobbin

The bobbin winder is situated at the right side of the machine beneath the top driving wheel. This is on the top of the machine table and has the winder wheel in front of the drive belt; adjoining is the bobbin shaft. Push the bobbin onto the shaft towards the small wheel as far as it will go. Follow the metal plate to the back of the machine where there is a tension wheel and thread guide. Then locate the thread spool holder further back; place the spool on this holder. Pass the thread through the hole in the guide, then through the centre of the tension discs. Bring it forward and round the bobbin on the bobbin shaft, winding the thread from the bottom to the top. Push the bobbin wheel forward to touch the drive belt. The lever that has been pushed forward must be between the two shoulders of the bobbin. (Figure 35).

It is important to keep the hands right away from the needle because the needle action cannot be stopped. Switch on the machine motor and add pressure to the foot plate with the feet to wind the bobbin. When the bobbin has sufficient thread wound, the lever will be pushed back by the

Thread guide and C. tension discs

Spool holder

B. Move left or right

A. Bobbin wheel

D. Regulating screw

amount of thread and so disengage the wheel from the belt to stop winding. (Figure 35, A).

Figure 35 Winding the bobbin

A bobbin can easily be wound while working embroidery, which will save some time when working on a large piece of embroidery. However, at this stage a bobbin is being wound before any work has been started. The machine has not been threaded and the hands must be kept away from the needle.

Adjusting the Bobbin Winder

If the thread has not been wound evenly on the bobbin, loosen the holding screw on the back tension bracket and move it left or right as required for corrections, then tighten the screw. (Figure 35, B).

If the thread is wound too loose or too tight, a correction can be made by adjusting the back tension nut. Turn this clockwise to tighten, anti-clockwise to loosen. (Figure 35, C).

If the bobbin is wound too full:

1. The bobbin will not fit in the bobbin case.

2. The surplus thread will fall off the bobbin and become tangled.

Adjust this by regulating the screw on the front thread lever. Turn the screw anti-clockwise to raise the thread lever; this will wind less thread onto the bobbin. Reverse the process if more thread is needed on the bobbin. (Figure 35, D).

17. Bobbin Case

Taking the Bobbin Case out

Diagram 25 Use the thumb and forefinger to pull the latch out towards the back of the machine

The bobbin case is found underneath the metal plate of the machine bed. Push the left-hand side of the plate out to the left; the bobbin case can now be seen through the plate hole. If the machine has a one-piece plate, this should be raised up and removed to see the bobbin case.

Use the left hand to reach the bobbin case latch. Go underneath the machine bed and to the back of the race (this is the underneath mechanism which revolves when the machine is in use). With the thumb and forefinger pull the latch out towards the back of the machine. Then pull the bobbin case backwards free from the machine by a firm hold on the latch. (Diagram 25).

While the latch is held open the bobbin will not fall out. As soon as the latch is released to its flat position, the bobbin is released and will fall out easily.

Bobbin Case Tension

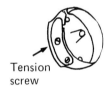

Tension screw

Diagram 26 Adjustable tension screw

On the outer edge of the case locate the thin metal band with two small screws; this is the tension lever. The far left end screw holds the tension lever in position, the second screw a little way in is the adjustable tension screw. Turn clockwise to tighten and anti-clockwise to loosen. (Diagram 26).

Threading the Bobbin Case

Hold the side edges of the bobbin case with the thumb and forefinger of the left hand with the round opening to the top and the tension lever facing the left. Take the bobbin in the right hand with the thumb and forefinger; have the thread coming from the top of the bobbin going to the left. Place the bobbin in the case. Locate the three slots in the edge of the case.

1. Take the thread through the far left first slot and pull the thread underneath the tension lever.

2. Take the thread down through the second slot, then

3. up through the third slot. (Diagram 27).

It may be found a little difficult to thread these last two slots, in which case loop the thread over the forefinger after the thread has been pulled under the tension lever and before it is taken down through the second slot.

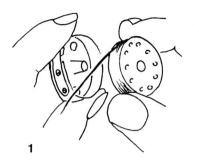 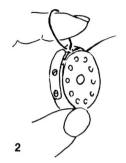 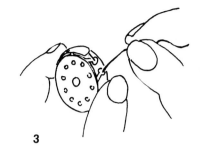

1   2   3

Bobbin Case In

Push open the left-hand side of the metal plate in the machine bed. Hold the bobbin case latch with the left hand between the thumb and forefinger. Move the thread that is coming out of the bobbin case at the top, then pull the length of thread over the back of the left hand. Now take the bobbin case underneath the bed of the machine to the back of the race. Locate the bobbin case shaft in the centre of the race and put the centre sleeve of the case onto the shaft. (Diagram 28). Push the case forward to the front of machine. Release the latch to lie flat; to make sure the bobbin case is secure pull the thread backwards. If the case falls out, repeat the process but push the bobbin case in a little harder.

Diagram 27
1. Thread from the top of bobbin going to the left
2. Thread taken through first slot and looped over finger for second and third slot
3. Thread going through the three slots of the bobbin case

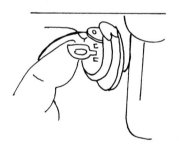

Diagram 28 Take the thread over the back of the left hand before replacing the bobbin case

18. Threading the Machine

The needle should be in a high position with the thread take-up lever in a high position as well.

1. Place the spool of thread on the top spool holder; pull the holder in an upright position to keep the spool in place while working.

2. To the immediate left of this there is an upright thread guide. Take the thread from the right to the left, first through the top hole and then through the lower hole.

3. To the left again there is a thread hole on the top of the front machine cover. Thread this from right to left.

4. Almost beneath this top thread hole is another in the machine housing. Thread this second one from left to right underneath the thread take-up lever.

5. Take the thread to the right and down through the centre of the top disc thread controller.

6. Below that and to the left slightly, locate the tension control disc; thread from right to left placing the thread between the two discs. Loop the thread over the right forefinger and push the thread spring guide to the right, thus making the thread loop over the hook attached to the disc housing and underneath the spring guide.

7. Just above the top left locate the wire thread guide; push the thread towards the machine housing and through the open end of the wire guide.

8. Take the thread up and go through the hole in the end of the take-up lever from right to left.

9. From the lever bring the thread down through the wire thread guide again.

10. Then through the round thread guide immediately below the wire.

11. Then through the wire coil thread guide immediately below the round tension control.

12. Beneath the coil and to the left locate the thread guide on the needle bar housing; slip the thread through the opening found to the back.

13. Beneath this, thread the round guide directly above the needle.

14. Thread the needle eye from the front to the back; leave a length of thread to the back of machine. (Figure 36a).

Top Tension

To adjust the top tension, which is the lower thread disc with the front spring and screw nut protruding, turn the screw nut to the left or anti-clockwise for a loose tension. Turn the screw nut to the right or clockwise for a tight tension. (Figure 36b).

The top and underneath tension should produce an equal stitch for straight running. For satin stitch the underneath thread should cover two-thirds of the width.

Figure 36 (a) To thread the top of the machine follow Nos 1–14.
  1. Top spool holder
  2. Thread guide
  3. Top thread hole
  4. Second hole
  5. Top disc
  6. Tension control
  7. Wire guide
  8. Take up lever
  9. Wire guide
  10. Round guide
  11. Wire coil
  12. Needle bar thread guide
  13. Round guide
  14. Needle

Figure 36 (b) Tension control: anti-clockwise for a loose tension, clockwise for a tight tension

Needle Sizes

The needle class number for the 107W 102 machine is 135 × 7; these are available in the old sizes: 9, 10, 11, 12, 14, 16, metric sizes: 60, 70, 80, 90, 100, 110.

It is important to use the correct size needle for the size thread that is being used. If a large needle is used for a fine thread it could distort the fabric. Always use an even thread such as a 50, 40, 36, a rayon twist or fine metal thread. A rough or uneven thread will not work with any success on this machine.

Changing the Needle

Release the screw located to the right of the needle bar; never take this right out. Remove the needle by pulling it downwards. The needle has a long groove on one side which is the front of the needle; the back has a small cut-out section at the thread eye. Push the needle up as far as it will go into the needle bar, with the long groove facing front. Then tighten the screw at the right of the needle bar to hold the needle in place.

19. Fabric

Almost any fabric can be used for embroidery on this machine, provided that the needle and thread size plus the tension have been adjusted to suit the type of embroidery being worked on the particular fabric. Jersey knit needs an extra firm hold while working, and the most difficult materials to use on this machine are leather and suede. These can be backed with an iron-on woven interlining which will directly stiffen the leather and suede, making it lose its supple quality. Tissue paper could be put underneath to help easy movement, and a very firm hold with the hands will help. However, a domestic machine fitted with a roller foot is more successful.

Always try a sample of embroidery on the material and make any adjustments necessary while working the sample before contemplating the finished piece of embroidery.

Holding the Fabric by Hand

The fabric must be held taut between the finger tips as it is being pushed underneath the needle. Hold the material either side of the needle and pull it taut outwards, always keeping the fingers close together and at least 2cm ($\frac{3}{4}$in) away from the needle. Use the finger tips with the knuckles up for the pushing movement, as though typing. This will give a free movement from the wrists. If the whole hand is in a flat position the movement made will be restricted and intermittent. (Figure 37).

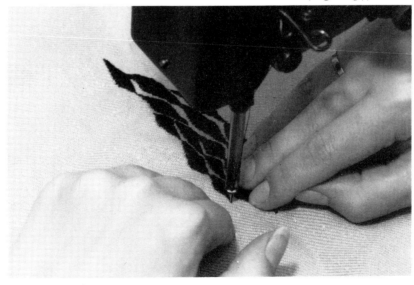

Figure 37 Hold material 2cm ($\frac{3}{4}$in) away from the needle and pull the material taut and outwards with the finger tips. Keep the fingers close together

Holding the Fabric in a Frame

The fabric could also be held tight in a round two-section embroidery frame; one section fits inside the outer larger section. If the frame is bound with fine fabric it will help stop any bruising of the fabrics being embroidered. The material must always be stretched on the straight grain. If this is distorted in any way the finished piece of work will always remain distorted. Move the fabric with the finger tips to obtain the free movement.

20.   Stitching

To Start Stitching

Before starting any work the underneath thread must always be brought to the top, through the material. Hold the top thread taut in the left hand directly to the back, while turning the top drive wheel forward. The needle must go down through the material and come back up again. As the needle comes up it will bring the underneath thread with it looped in the top thread. Pull the underneath thread through the material to lay on the top. Hold both threads underneath the fingers until the first few stitches have been worked. After the threads have been secured in this way they can be cut off close to the surface of the material. Place the needle down in the fabric, position the hands, then add pressure to the foot plate to start work. Always commence working in this order, then there will be no movement of the fabric as the hands are positioned.

Straight Stitch

Try the straight stitch running in various directional movements to get used to the movements of the hands with the speed of the machine. Also

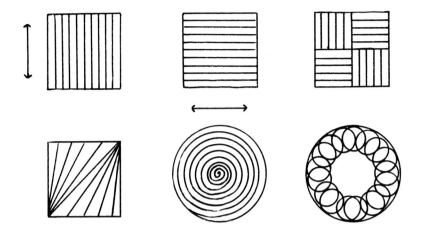

Diagram 29 Work different directional movements to gain co-ordination

try to keep the stitch length the same and the distance between each line the same. Draw some shapes onto the fabric and fill each shape with a different directional movement. (Diagram 29). Always put the needle down into the fabric before commencing any work and hold the two ends of thread. Control the speed of the machine with the feet on the foot plate, while moving the fabric with the hands to make an even stitch.

Fastening Off

By working a few stitches on the same spot the threads will be fastened off. The threads can then be cut off close to the surface of the material.

Knee Bar

The knee bar plate is located underneath the machine bed just to the right. (Figure 38). This should be easy to push out and return with the right knee touching the bar at its centre. If the knee bar is too high or too low it can be adjusted up or down on the shaft by loosening the nut at the back of the knee bar plate. After adjusting, the nut must be tightened to hold the knee bar firm. As the knee bar is pushed out with the right knee the needle bar will swing its action from right to left and produce a zigzag stitch. The width is regulated by the pressure on the knee bar and can vary from a straight stitch to the full width of 13mm ($\frac{1}{2}$in).

Figure 38 Knee bar, showing the adjusting nut to move it up or down. As the knee bar is pushed out to the right with the right knee, the needle bar will swing from left to right and so work the stitch width to a full 13mm ($\frac{1}{2}$in)

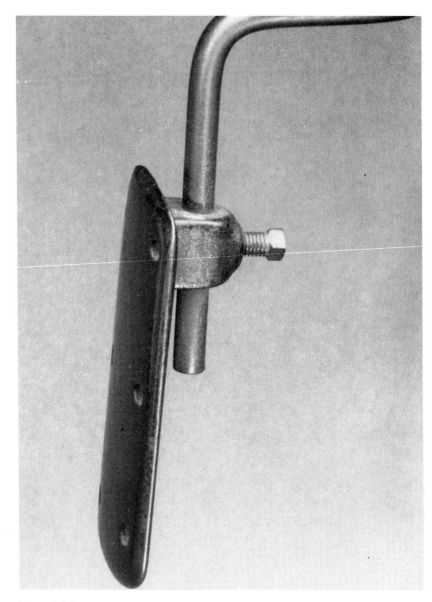

Diagrams 30 & 31, below. Co-ordinate the hand movement. (Left) Hand movement too fast with a slow speed. (Right) Hand movement too slow with a fast speed

Hand Movement

To work a continuous satin stitch, the hand movement must be very precise when pushing the work through. If the hand movement is too quick with a slow speed of the machine, the result will be a zigzag. (Diagram 30). If the hand movement is too slow with a fast speed of the machine, the result will be a build up of satin stitches being worked on top of each other. (Diagram 31). The hand movement and the speed of the machine must be worked in co-ordination to obtain a smooth satin stitch. Always work to the outside of the design lines for a professional finish, otherwise the finished work will have a line all round the edge.

21. Continuous Width

Setting the Width

At the centre back of the machine there is a numbered scale bar to show the different grades available for the width. As pressure is added to the knee bar the numbered scale bar will move to the right and show a low to higher number for a small to wide zigzag throw. To the back of the scale bar locate the large thumb nut; when this is turned to the right it will tighten onto the numbered scale bar and hold it firm in a selected position. (Figure 39).

Draw a straight line on the fabric; this will be a guide for the centre of the set stitch. Bring the underneath thread to the top and hold both threads on the fabric; put the needle down in the fabric 1cm (⅜in) from the top of the drawn line. Make straight running stitches to the top of the line. As the top is reached add pressure to the knee bar which will give a zigzag. (Diagram 32). When the required width has been reached hold the pressure on the knee bar. Take the pressure off the foot plate to stop the machine working; the needle must be down in the work either side of the zigzag. Hold the work level with the left hand, while keeping the exact pressure on the knee bar. Tighten the large thumb nut by reaching over the top of the machine with the right hand. This may seem a very complicated action, but after setting the stitch a few times it will become easier.

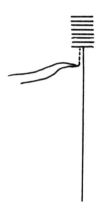

Diagram 32 Vertical movement. Add pressure to the knee bar for the width

Figure 39 Tighten the large thumb nut at the back of the machine to obtain a set width stitch

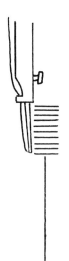

Satin Stitch

The machine is now set to work a continuous width as previously set. Keep the drawn line in the centre of the satin stitch while working. (Diagram 32). Also co-ordinate the hand movement with the speed of the machine to produce a smooth satin stitch. When the machine has to be stopped to move the hand position, the needle must be left in the material either side of the satin stitch before repositioning the hands. (Diagram 33). If the needle is left out, the material could easily be moved and so distort a straight line. For a curve always leave the needle in the fabric on the outer edge of the curve to eliminate any triangular gaps in the satin stitch.

Fastening Off

Diagram 33 Leave the needle down in the material before repositioning the hands

Figure 40 Long and short stitch worked with a horizontal movement and colour change to produce shading

The satin stitch must be fastened off to secure the ends of the thread, otherwise the stitches will easily unravel. One quick method is to work a few straight stitches on the spot in the centre or one side of the satin stitch. Then cut the ends off close to the surface of the material. The second method is to leave a length of the top and underneath threads. Take the top thread to the underneath and with a sewing needle oversew three stitches in the back of the satin stitch. The second method will take longer.

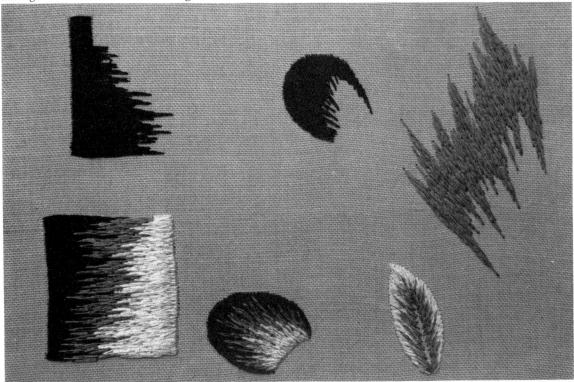

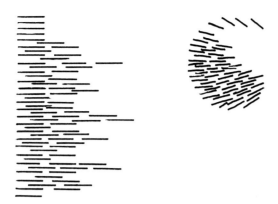

Diagram 34 Horizontal movement for long and short stitch. The long and short stitches interlock

Long and Short

Long and short can be used as a filling technique for areas or shapes. The stitch is set for a width but instead of moving the fabric in a vertical movement it is moved horizontally. The stitches are interlocked; first make a long sideways movement and then a short movement. (Diagram 34). Avoid any hard vertical stitch lines in the movements as they protrude in the stitching and distort the flow of the horizontal stitches. Shading can easily be worked by changing the thread colour. (Figure 40). The stitches should cover the fabric; however, they should never be too solid and so produce a piece of embroidery that is too stiff.

22. Continuous Movement

The continuous movement of the knee bar is used for direct control when working the varying shapes. These would be, for example, spots, petal shapes, shaped edges and lettering. This way the machine can be used to its full capacity with ease for an unlimited variety of shapes.

The machine could also be used as for set stitch satin with much more directional hand movements. This method will rely on how the fabric is moved to create the shapes, not the knee bar movement.

Varying Shapes: I

Using the machine for shapes with the knee bar, the work can be pushed backwards, forwards or diagonally. The pressure put on the knee bar is in co-ordination with the hand movement, the speed of the machine and the reading of the design.

For the straightforward petal shape, take a running stitch to the point. Add slight pressure to the knee bar for the point. As the shape gets wider gradually add more pressure to the knee bar until the widest section has been worked, then gradually ease the pressure on the knee bar to come back to the lower point. Once the easier shapes have been mastered the more complex shapes with hand turning as well as the knee bar movement can be tried, as well as the diagonal filling of shapes; for this the design is held at a slant and the material is pushed through at a slight angle. (Figure 41).

Varying Shapes: II

The second method of varying shapes will rely on the skilful continuous movement of the fabric by the hands. The machine is set to the required width, the fabric is moved diagonally for a narrow stitch and straight back for the wide stitch. Complete awareness of the diagonal and straight

Figure 41 Continuous movement. From left to right the sections of the photo show: Knee bar movement with the hand movement straight; Knee bar movement with the hand movement diagonal; Knee bar movement with the hand movement diagonal and straight; Set stitch movement with the hand movement diagonal and straight

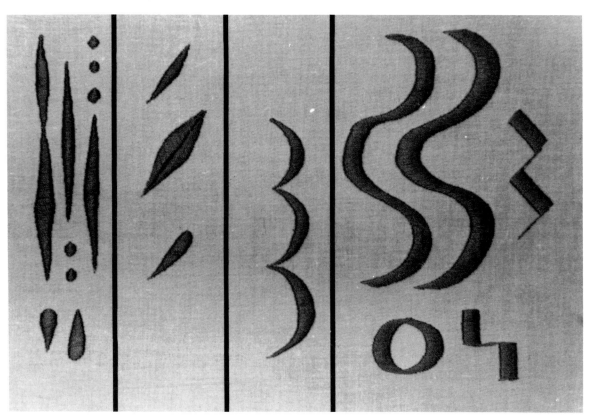

movements are needed for this method in order to produce the varying shapes. (Figure 41). Finish off the ends as for set stitch by working a few straight running stitches, or take the top thread to the back of the material and oversew through the worked stitch line.

 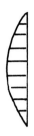  

Diagram 35 The back punch as seen from the back of the machine

Diagram 36 A left side shape, the same amount of shape either side of a central line, and a right side shape

Back Punch

The back punch can be seen protruding above the centre of the machine arm, directly above the set stitch mechanism. (Diagram 35). This has three positions in the centre hole; the machine will work the same amount either side of a central line when the knee bar has pressure added. If the plunger is put in the right hand hole and pressure is added to the knee bar, the stitch will shape to the right side and have a straight line on the left. If the plunger is put in the left-hand hole and pressure is added to the knee bar the stitch will shape to the left side and have a straight line to the right. (Diagram 36).

To move the plunger lever pull the small round knob straight back; this will release the plunger from its previous position. Then move sideways to the desired hole on the left or right and ensure that the plunger is secured as far as it will go in its new position. After the work has been completed move the plunger back to its central position for equal shape from the centre.

Lettering

For lettering it is advisable to place the fabric in the round embroidery frame to alleviate distortion with the hand positioning. This can easily happen if a very soft or slippery fabric such as satin is being used. If a very firm fabric is to be used the frame may not be necessary. The knee bar movement and the set stitch movement can be used for lettering. (Figure 42). This will require extreme accuracy to achieve a good clear line; if the lettering is on a very small scale the end result could well be incomprehensible.

This technique usually has a slight pad to give a round, soft satin finish. A shadow effect could also be added by the side of the lettering with a running or fine satin stitch.

Figure 42 Lettering. The
knee bar movement was used
for the letter A with a
running stitch shadow line.
The knee bar movement was
used for the letter B with a
satin stitch shadow line. A set
stitch was used for the letter
C. All the letters were
padded with a running stitch
first, then the satin stitch was
worked over the running
stitch

23. Padded Satin

This will give a raised satin stitch; it can be used for the set stitch and for the varying shapes. The padding is worked first, then the satin stitch is worked over the padding. It can be padded with wool, cord, string, thread or felt. If a very hard padding is used the finished work could be very stiff, therefore the suitability of the padding for the embroidery must be considered. The design for the padded satin should not have any crossing over of lines. It is impossible to work a smooth satin through a cord at the crossover section. Design or make an adaption to a design for the padded satin to be side-by-side. (Diagram 37).

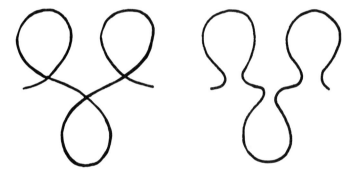

Diagram 37 Padded satin. The design on the left is not suitable for a padded satin if using a cord or string for the padding, but the adaptation (right) to the design would be suitable

Set Stitch

For a slight pad in the centre of a set stitch design, work a few rows of running stitch. It will depend on the width of the satin as to how many rows are worked. For a narrow satin it may be four, if it is wide ten running stitch rows may be needed. Never work the padding out as far as the finished width edge; always keep just inside of the finished edge.

For a high pad in the centre of the set stitch design, couch down wool, cord or string with a zigzag stitch. Again, it will depend on how high the padding is needed as to what is used. A cord could be couched over a wool or a string over a cord if more depth is needed.

The finished satin stitch is worked over the padding, and in covering the design lines make sure the padding is completely covered, for a professional finish. (Figure 43).

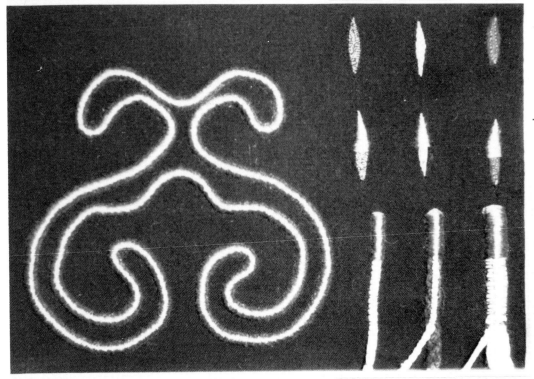

Running stitch pad

Long and short stitch pad

Felt pad

Satin stitch worked over half of the shape and part of the cord

Cord pad

Thin cord on top of a wool cord

Thin cord or string on top of a thick cord

Figure 43 The design on the left of the photo shows set stitch worked over a cord padding

Shapes

To obtain a slight pad in the centre of the shape, work rows of running stitch, keeping to the inside of the design lines.

For a high pad use felt cut to the required shape. Ensure that this fits inside the design line. Stitch the felt around the outside edge within the design lines.

The finished satin stitch is worked over the padding to cover the design line and the padding. It is advisable to use the same colour padding material as that of the thread used for the finished stitch. (Figure 43).

Large Areas

If larger areas are to be padded this could be worked using the trapunto method of padding.

Work all the satin stitch areas needed on single fabric. Then place a piece of fabric across the back of this and work a running stitch around the satin stitch areas that are to be padded. Securely fasten off all the ends. Work from the back and thread wool or push the padding in to fill the area between the back material and the front embroidery.

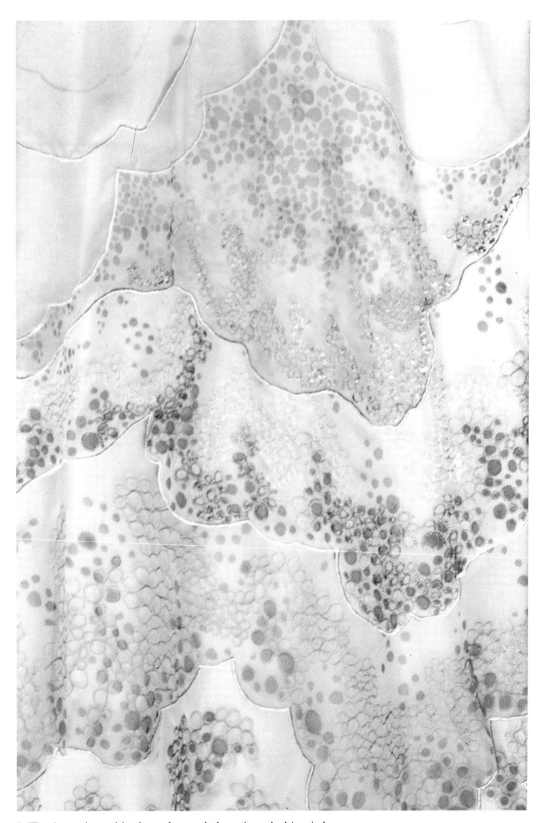

3. The domestic machine is used to work the satin and whip stitches

4. The tambour method of work is used here for cut out,
sandwich padding and beading

24. Adjusting Tension

Metal Thread

There are now two ways of working gold thread on this machine. The fine round lurex thread available can be used for the top thread to work a fine delicate line easily on a satin stitch. The thicker gold threads such as jap, which is a slightly flat thread, and the flat lurex, are wound onto the bobbin for working the reverse way. Therefore the tension adjustments are different for whichever thread and method is being employed.

Fine lurex thread

The fine lurex thread is used on top of the machine; the threading is the same as previously explained. For this the top tension must be medium to loose, which will help prevent the lurex from splitting. The bobbin can be wound with the lurex thread; for this adjust the bobbin case for a medium to loose tension. The bobbin could also be wound with thread, for which the tension should be medium. Use the machine as for normal working from the right side, but first try a sample and adjust the tensions if they are

Figure 44 Metal thread. Fine lurex thread used on the top of the machine and worked on the right side of the material. Medium to loose top tension. Flat lurex and jap threads are wound onto the bobbin and worked on the wrong side of the material. Medium to loose bobbin case tension with a tight top tension

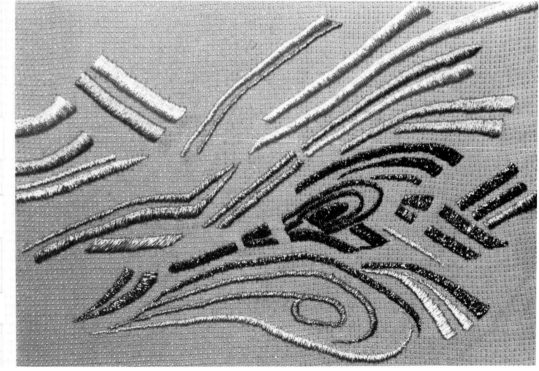

Fine
lurex
thread

Flat
lurex
thread

Jap
thread

93

not correct. This thread may not work satisfactorily if the machine is used to its maximum speed, in which case keep the speed to medium. (Figure 44).

Jap and flat lurex thread

Using the jap and lurex threads the working is reversed and worked from the wrong side. The design is traced onto the wrong side of the work, and if lettering or assymmetric designs are being used they must be reversed before tracing onto the wrong side. On completion of the embroidery the work is turned over and the design elements will then be visually correct.

These metal threads are wound onto the bobbin. The bobbin case tension should be adjusted for medium to loose. The jap and lurex threads are pulled through the fabric so that they just show on the wrong side. Use a strong 40 thread on the top and have a tighter than normal top tension. (Figure 44).

Movement

As these threads are a little thicker than ordinary 50 thread, the hand movement must be correct for the spacing of the stitches and must allow the jap and lurex threads to lie flat. Try a sample and note that the metal threads must cover the underneath completely so that no 40 thread is visible on the right side. Also be aware of the shaping and keep the movement even to ensure that a build-up of stitches will not occur. Adjust the tensions where necessary to produce a professional finish.

Wool

A fine two-ply wool is advisable for use on this machine; it should be smooth and supple. If the wool has a wiry element it will be very difficult to achieve a satisfactory result. A wool with a long hair finish such as angora or mohair will tangle with the revolution of the bobbin. These are far better couched from the top. The fine two-ply wool is used in the same way as previously explained for the jap and lurex threads, and worked from the back.

Tension

The wool is wound onto the bobbin with the bobbin case tension loose. Never have this tension screw too loose for the screw to fall out while working. (These screws are very difficult to find). If it is impossible to obtain a tension loose enough, have a piece of white paper on the table and then take the tension bar completely off. Fold the two screws and the tension bar in the paper and put these somewhere safe for later use.

The top should have a strong 36 thread to hold the wool as it is pulled through the fabric. A tighter than normal adjustment is made to the top tension.

Movement

As the wool is thicker than a 50 thread and the metal threads, the hand movement for the spacing of the stitches should be a little further apart. Adjustments can be made at the sample stage for this and also to the tensions. The wool must completely cover the stitch area on the right side; no top thread should be visible at the sides of the satin stitch. (Figure 45).

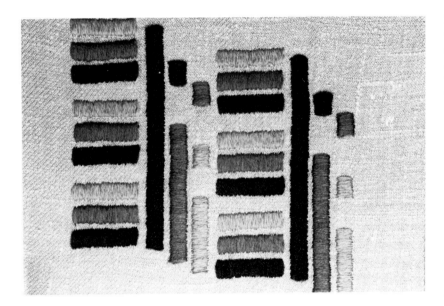

Figure 45 Wool wound onto the bobbin and worked on the wrong side of the material. Medium to loose bobbin case tension with a tight top tension

Couching

For angora or mohair wool use the same colour thread as the wool for the top and underneath. Adjust the machine to normal tensions and use a running stitch. Hold the wool in the left hand onto the right side of the fabric, then couch down in position with a sideways stitch. Move the wool and hold it to the left – this will avoid stitching the long hairs of the wool – then run stitch further along the design line, but not more than 1 cm ($\frac{3}{8}$in). Then bring the wool from the left back onto the design line and couch it in position with a sideways stitch. Repeat this process to complete the design line or use this process to work a solid filling in one area. After the couching has been completed take the ends of the wool through to the back of the fabric and oversew to the wrong side of stitching. (Figure 46).

This method can also be used for couching multiple wool ends. The individual wool end is couched and then twisted with the other wool ends to form a straightforward cord twist to the more elaborate twists or to form loops.

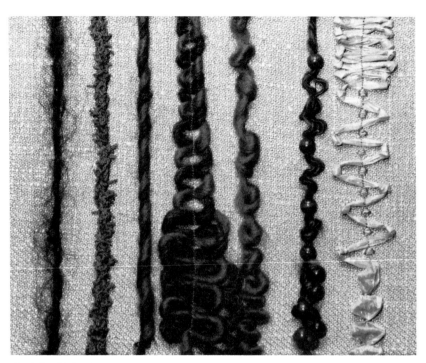

Figure 46 Couching. From left to right the photo shows: Mohair; Novelty loop thread; Twisted wool (and an alternative method of couching it); Knotted wool; Wool knotted and looped while couching with beads; Raffeine knotted and looped

Cable Stitch

A thicker thread such as a perlé, Anchor soft or a silky crochet thread is wound onto the bobbin. The embroidery is worked from the wrong side as for jap thread and the wool coming from the bobbin; adjust both the tensions for this method.

This stitch can be worked to give a really chunky effect or a smooth surface. To achieve the raised chunky effect work with a straight stitch but move the fabric to make very small circles; these circles can be side-by-side or overlap each other. The smooth cable stitch is achieved by working the straight running stitch in lines side-by-side or a width to produce the satin stitch. If working the satin stitch allow for the thicker thread with the movements, so that the thread will lie side-by-side and not overlap the previous stitch. (Figure 47).

If the intention is to combine the cable stitch with a fine satin stitch and the majority of the embroidery is to be worked from the right side, trace the design onto the right side of the fabric. Use a fine thread and normal tensions to work a straight running stitch round the areas that are to be worked in the cable stitch and, if possible, use the same colour thread as the cable thread. This will outline the areas for the cable stitch and mark the design through to the wrong side of the fabric for the cable stitch method. Adjust the machine tensions for working from the wrong side and work the cable stitch first from the wrong side, to be chunky or to give a smooth effect. Finish all the cable stitch areas off first, then the work can be turned over and the tensions adjusted back to normal for the complete design to be finished from the right side of the fabric.

96

Figure 47 Cable stitch. The grey background lines and the foliage on the trees are perlé thread worked with a satin stitch, while the darker undergrowth is lacet braid worked with a running stitch

Figure 48 Whip stitch, worked with a rayon twist, flat lurex and a thread in a straight running stitch and continuous circles

Whip Stitch

This stitch has the same tension adjustments as the jap thread, wool and the cable stitch: a tight top tension and a loose underneath tension. The difference with the whip stitch is that it is worked from the right side of the fabric. A fine thread is used in the bobbin and this is pulled through the fabric to whip the top thread. This produces a small bead or a top loop effect which is over the top thread. If the top tension is too tight with a very loose underneath tension the bead or loop will be larger on the right side of the fabric. To obtain a more interesting stitch use a contrast colour thread underneath to that on the top and move the fabric with intermittent spacing. Where there are small stitches the underneath contrast thread will be more prominent. The longer stitches will show the top thread more, with the contrast underneath thread at intervals in between. If the interest in the design is to be produced by the contrast colour, then there should be complete control of the stitching by the movements made of the fabric; this .needs to be precise.

The same colour can be used for the top and the underneath. However, for the full effect use a thread with a gloss such as a rayon twist or a metal thread in the bobbin, and a dull thread on the top. To produce a more textured effect work a straight running stitch in continuous circles, starting very small and gradually getting larger. (Figure 48). For covering an area work a straight running stitch in fairly large circles just touching each other; this will produce a spiked effect.

25.   Techniques

Appliqué

This is the addition of one fabric onto another or onto a ground fabric for small or large areas. A plain, printed, decorated or velvet fabric can be used for this method. The woven fabric can be applied from the top or the underneath, depending on the design.

Different fabrics

For working a design that is to have different fabrics or colours applied to one piece of work, trace the design onto the wrong side of the ground fabric. Remember if using an assymmetric design that this should be reversed before tracing. It is also very important to remember that the straight grain of both the applied and the ground fabric must be in the same direction. Always have the fabric flat at this stage. Before applying any fabric iron it to remove crease lines. Place the fabric that is to be applied onto the right side of the ground fabric; it must be large enough to cover the section of the appliqué area and to cover the design line. Check the straight grain lines are in the same direction, then tack or pin the appliqué piece in position to hold this firm while working. If using pins these must be well outside the design line and away from the needle action.

A thread, rayon twist or metal thread can be used for this work. Set the machine to work a narrow width and work a zigzag around the area to be applied. Then turn the work over to the right side and cut the surplus fabric away close to the zigzag stitch around the outside of the applied section. Apply all the different fabrics in this way until all the appliqué pieces have been stitched in position.

After all the pieces of fabric have been applied and cut out the top stitching can be worked. Finish the appliqué stitching from the right side, working over the zigzag stitch with a slightly wider satin stitch. This could be either a set satin stitch, a padded satin stitch or satin stitch with movement from narrow to wide. The finished piece of embroidery must not show any raw edges of the fabric or any zigzag stitches. (Figure 49).

Figure 49 Appliqué. Different colours of fabric applied with the design traced onto the wrong side of the ground fabric and the appliqué fabric pinned to the right side. Keep the grain of both fabrics going in the same direction

One piece appliqué

Trace the design onto the right side of the fabric that is to be used for the appliqué. This is put in position onto the right side of the ground fabric and held in place with the pins or a tacking stitch. If a very large piece of appliqué is to be worked then a cross tack through the centre is advisable to help stop any movement while working. Proceed as explained previously: zigzag, cut out and then work the finishing stitch over the edge of the fabric and the zigzag. (Figure 50).

Sandwich appliqué

For this use the appliqué method with the addition of a third layer, such as acetate or leather, which is sandwiched between the ground fabric and

Figure 50 One piece appliqué.
Painted fabric placed onto the
right side of the ground
fabric

Figure 51 Sandwich appliqué.
A fine organza was used to
sandwich the acetate

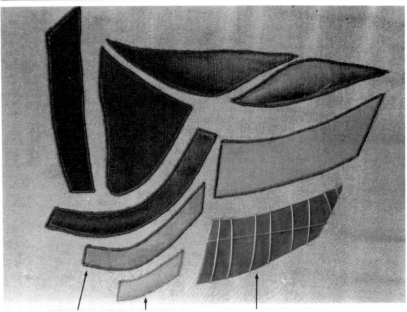

Finished   Material over the shape   Acetate tacked in position
satin stitch   with the first zigzag line

a see-through appliqué fabric. In this way the shine of the acetate or
leather will show through the appliqué fabric.

Trace the design onto the top of the ground fabric. Use a tracing paper
and trace round the shape which is to have the third layer. This must be
just inside the design line so that sufficient room is left for the width of the
satin stitch. Place this shape onto the acetate or leather and cut round as
though using a template. Tack the acetate or leather shape in position by
taking the stitches right over the shape from one side to the other; never
stitch through this as it will mark. These tacks must be accessible from

the back of the ground fabric because after all the satin stitch has been completed the tacks are taken out. Place the see-through appliqué over the second layer of shapes and proceed as for the appliqué method, after which remove the tacking from the second layer. (Figure 51).

Cut Work

For the technique of cut work the ground fabric is cut away to produce a scalloped edge, or cut away between embroidered shapes similar to Broderie Anglaise, where the design has small shapes. The addition of worked bars will be needed if the cut-out shapes are large in size. These bars are worked across the cut shape to avoid any distortion. This technique is the same for all fabrics that are going to be cut away.

Small shapes

Use a vanishing muslin as a backing; this will hold the ground fabric in place when working on the edge. There are two ways of tracing: if using white fabric trace on the vanishing muslin and for a coloured fabric trace on the right side. This is suggested because white always marks so easily that the tracing may be difficult to remove if it is not completely covered with stitching. Work a straight running stitch on the design line where the areas are to be cut out. This will be from the back on the white fabric and from the front on the coloured fabrics. Then from the right side work a very narrow zigzag over the straight running stitch line; this must be smaller in width than the final stitch width.

A very sharp pair of small scissors will be required to cut away the inner shapes or the surplus fabric from a scallop edge. Do not cut through the vanishing muslin as this will hold the shapes in place when working the final stitch line. After the cutting away has been finished work a set satin stitch or a shaped satin stitch over the zigzag and the straight running stitch. The satin stitch must cover both the zigzag and the cut edge of the fabric. (Figure 52).

It is important to work the straight running stitch as this will hold the shapes in place, especially when working on the cross grain of the fabric.

Eyelet

One method of working an eyelet is the continuous movement by turning the fabric round in a circle. This will have the same width all the way round the eyelet. The second method has a very narrow top and lower edge, with wider sides. These can be worked as for the cut-out method, or completely finished and the holes punched out afterwards with a round punch.

The turned eyelet is more successful with frequent stops to turn the fabric. Leave the needle in on the outside of the eyelet curve, turn the fabric slightly before working a few more stitches and also turn the fabric while working a little further round the eyelet. Then stop to turn the

1. Running stitch worked on the design line

2. Small zigzag worked over the running stitch

3. Cut out section of fabric

4. Finish the edge with satin stitch

Figure 52 Cut work

fabric again after a few stitches have been worked. These stitches must radiate from the inner circle all the way round the eyelet. (Figure 53).

For the second method there is no continual turning round of the fabric. The top has a sideways movement, producing stitches simulating stem stitch. Then move the fabric backwards and curve right to produce the first quarter. Curve left to the lower edge and make a sideways movement for the simulated stem stitch for the lower edge and half of the eyelet. To complete the circle move the fabric forward and curve to the left for the three quarters, then curve right to meet the top sideways stitches. (Figure 53).

Padded cut work

This method is worked the same way as cut work to the zigzag stitching stage of the process, except that when working this zigzag, couch down a padding as for padded satin stitch instead of working the flat zigzag. After this the finishing is the same as for the cut work. Cover the padding and the raw edge of the fabric with a set satin stitch.

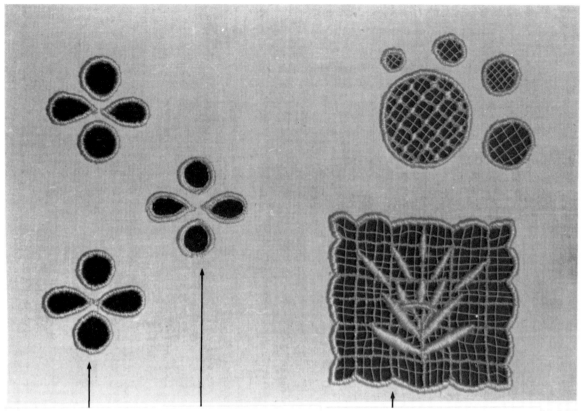

These shapes are turned round while working. No vanishing muslin and cut out before the satin stitch finish

These shapes are not turned. No vanishing muslin and cut out after the satin stitch finish

After the cut out stage has been completed work the centre thread mesh. The centre mesh can be worked on with shapes a set stitch or couching.

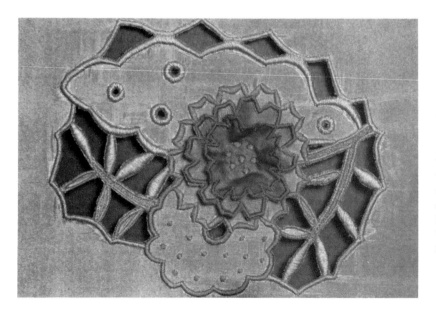

Above

Figure 53 Working eyelets (left) and open work (right)

Figure 54 Layer cut shapes. Work all the cut out sections as for cut work. The loose flower is worked on a separate piece of fabric. The loose flower could be worked using the same method as cut work or worked to the final satin stitch edge and then cut out last. After the flower has been cut out it is applied to the ground fabric with a running or a satin stitch

103

Open work

The open work has an open embroidered centre surrounded by fabric. A mesh is worked in the cut-out centre open space, after which it can be embroidered.

Trace the design onto vanishing muslin and place this on the wrong side of the fabric. The use of vanishing muslin is advisable for a large area of open work as it will help to make the work easier; however, this method can be worked with the fabric held taut in the round frame.

Work to the zigzag and cut-out stage as previously explained; do not finish the cut outer edge until the centre section has been completed. Use a straight running stitch to work the centre mesh from one side to another across the open area. Both ends of each line must be attached securely to the zigzag edge on the fabric. Once all the mesh has been completed, the satin stitch shapes, set stitch or couching can be embroidered onto the mesh ground. If the mesh is very open and satin shapes are to be added it would help to have a foundation to work over. First work the shapes with close lines of running stitch crossing over each other within the shape to make the foundation, and then satin stitch over that for the finished stitching. (Figure 53). The set satin stitch can alternatively be worked over the straight lines of the mesh; these can be built up as a foundation as previously explained for a wide satin stitch (p. 92). After the central piece has been completed the outer edge of the fabric is finished off with a satin stitch. This must cover all the secured running stitch lines and the edge of the fabric.

Figure 55 All these shapes were worked to the satin stitch stage, cut out last and then applied to the ground fabric

Layer padded cut work

For this technique three layers of fabric are used: the top layer, which is cut to reveal the second fabric, and the third fabric to hold the padding in position. It is the padding combined with the cut sections that add interest to these layers. The top cut fabric is raised to show the second

layer of fabric by the padding. The design will need two lines on the sections that are to be cut. (Figure 56).

Figure 56 Layer padded cut work. The inner line of the cut section is worked first

The design is traced onto the right side of the top fabric. On this single fabric only work the inner line of the cut section; finish with a narrow set stitch and cut away the floating threads that are on both sides. Place the second and third fabrics underneath the top fabric; these must be large enough to cover the design. Now work through the three layers of fabric to complete the design stitching.

Cut through the top layer of fabric only, between the two close satin stitch lines. Turn the work to the back and push the padding through the third layer of fabric, as with trapunto padding, to lie between the second and third fabrics in the padded sections of the design. (Figure 56).

Stitched bars

If the cut-out shapes are large they will not retain the original shapes once the backing has been removed. The worked bars will overcome this problem when they are worked at intervals across the open shape.

After the cut-out stage has been worked use the straight running stitch to work four lines close together across the shape. Attach the lines securely to the zigzag at either side of the cut-out shape, after which work a narrow set satin stitch over the running stitch lines. This is the worked bar which should be placed at intervals 1cm ($\frac{3}{8}$in) along the open cut shape.

The finished satin edge on the shape is worked after all the bars have been completed. This finishing edge will then cover the running stitch between the worked bars, plus the zigzag and the edge of the material. (Figure 57).

2. Small zigzag worked over the running stitch — 1. Running stitch worked on the design line

3. Cut out section of fabric and a running stitch
   is worked as a base to hold the satin stitch bars

4. When all the bars have been completed
   finish the outer edge

Figure 57 Stitched bars

Vanishing Muslin

On the completion of the embroidery the vanishing muslin can be ironed off. Set the iron temperature to that of the fabric attached to the vanishing muslin. Place the right side of the embroidery down onto a slightly padded surface. Iron the vanishing muslin until it turns a light brown in colour; keep the iron moving over the surface of the vanishing muslin the whole time. After all the vanishing muslin has turned a light brown it can be rubbed away or brushed off; never use a sharp implement for this as it could easily tear the fabric. The round handle of a pair of scissors is extremely useful for this. Give the embroidery a final press on the wrong side after all the muslin has been cleaned away.

Evenweave

There are different techniques that can be used with evenweave fabrics. One is drawn thread, where the threads are withdrawn in one direction

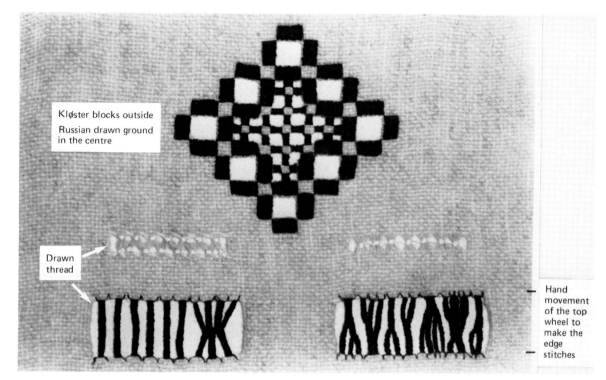

Kløster blocks outside
Russian drawn ground
in the centre

Drawn thread

Hand movement of the top wheel to make the edge stitches

and stitching worked over the threads that remain. Threads can also be withdrawn from the warp and the weft to simulate Russian drawn ground; the stitching is worked over the threads that remain in both directions. Solid blocks of set satin stitch similar to the Kløster blocks used in Hardanger are worked on the counted thread basis. An imitation of blackwork on the counted threads could also be worked with a straight running stitch.

Drawn thread

After sufficient threads have been withdrawn in one direction set the machine for the width required; this is calculated by the number of threads that are to be stitched together. This method is easier and more under control if the fabric is held tight at the top and bottom of the threads that are being stitched over. After the first bar has been stitched secure the end threads by stitching over a few threads of the ground fabric. To accomplish this, move the top wheel and the work by hand; as the machine is left in its set position co-ordinate the movements. Make a stitch over a few threads of the ground fabric then come back to work the adjoining bar. (Figure 58). The appearance of this stitch will be similar to hem stitching at each end of the worked bars.

If you are taking the threads out in both directions leave some threads in at alternate intervals; for instance, pull out three, leave in three, pull out the next three. The threads left in are worked over in both directions, or worked over with a running stitch to link the threads together. The

Figure 58 Even weave. The Kløster blocks are worked using a satin stitch keeping to the grain of the fabric and cut out last. The threads are removed for the Russian drawn ground and the remaining threads worked over using a satin stitch. For drawn thread the threads are removed from the horizontal grain and the remaining vertical threads worked over using a satin stitch.

outer edge can be finished with blocks of satin stitch where the threads have been cut, or with a satin stitch all the way round.

Kløster blocks

The solid blocks to simulate Kløster blocks are worked over the threads by counting the required numbers to be worked over. If the satin stitch covers six threads then work over six threads down for a square, or more threads down for an oblong. If the blocks are worked to form a square or oblong shape, the enclosed centre can then be cut out. (Figure 58).

Counted pattern

To work the simulated blackwork use the straight running stitch. Count the threads that are to be worked over to form the stitch pattern. For a heavy close area work over less threads and for a thin or light area work over more threads. (Figure 59).

Figure 59 Blackwork. This is worked by counting the threads and using a running stitch. For the light areas work one line, for the heavy areas work two or three lines

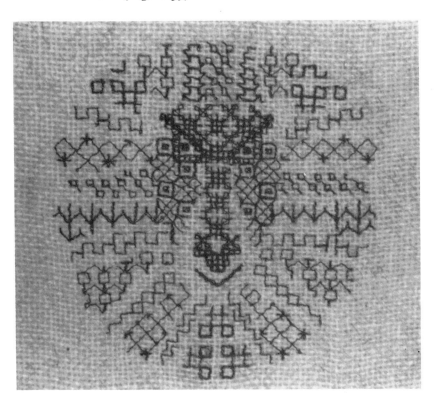

Shadow

The shadow in this instance is with the use of transparent fabric when using one, two or more layers for a different density with one colour fabric, or transparent fabric with many different colours. The most effective fabric for this is organza; a chiffon is very flexible and may prove to be a difficult fabric to use.

Trace the design onto the right side of the ground fabric as this is to be worked from the right side. The different layers or colours of fabric are placed underneath the ground piece, therefore one density or one colour should be stitched through at each stage to avoid any mistakes. Always try the shadow colour underneath the ground fabric beforehand as there may be some colour distortion, especially if using a dark colour for the ground fabric. For this a better result will be achieved if bright, vibrant shadow colours are used under a dark ground fabric. With the resulting shadow the colours retain their interest but with a subtle effect.

One colour

If using layers of one colour place the maximum number of layers at the back and use a fine zigzag to stitch the selected shapes for this density. Turn the work over and cut away the surplus fabric from one layer only, around the zigzag shapes from the wrong side. Turn back to the right side and zigzag the selected shapes for the slightly less dense areas. Turn the work over and cut away one more layer of surplus fabric from the wrong side. Continue in this manner until only the single layer areas remain and all the surplus fabric has been cut away. To complete the embroidery, work a set satin stitch or a shaped satin stitch over the zigzag lines. This method will produce a design containing the areas of varying density. Some areas could also be cut out completely to give another dimension. (Figure 60).

Different colour

The contrast colour shadow is executed in the same way as for the single colour shadow. Lay one colour at a time under the ground fabric, work a zigzag around the shapes and cut away the surplus fabric from the back. Then lay the second colour underneath and proceed in the same manner until all the colours are in place. When the design is complete finish off the

Figure 60 Shadow. The design on the left is one colour shadow with three, two and one layers of fabric. Different colour shadow is shown on the right

embroidery with a satin stitch. Again, if required, some of the shapes could be cut out completely, depending on the design. (Figure 60).

Fringe

The fringe can be worked by two different methods: either using a fine thread and satin stitch, or couching a thicker thread to a heavy wool with a straight running stitch. The length can vary from 5mm to 150mm ($\frac{1}{4}$–6in) with a loop edge or cut for a straight edge.

Short fine fringe

For the fine satin stitch fringe, thread the machine with a rayon twist, metal thread or thread. Adjust the top tension for medium to loose and check that the underneath thread is only covering a quarter to half the full width of the satin stitch. Set the machine to the width required; the finished length of the fringe will be the set width plus one quarter. The maximum length is governed by the fullest width obtainable, on this machine, of 13mm ($\frac{1}{2}$in) plus one quarter, to make a 16mm ($\frac{5}{8}$in) fringe. After the machine has been set, first work a fairly close satin stitch. Secondly, work a very narrow set stitch over one side edge of the wider satin stitch. Thirdly, turn the work to the wrong side and carefully pull out the underneath thread from the wider satin stitch only. Turn back to the right side; the free side edge of the satin stitch must be eased out from the fabric to lie on the top. This is the fine fringe; it can be left with the loops for the fringe ends or be cut to form a straight edge. (Figure 61).

Figure 61 Short fringe. (Left) Right side finished, the wide and narrow satin stitch. (Top Centre) Wrong side, with the underneath thread removed from the wide satin stitch only. (Right) Right side, the finished short fringe left with the loops for the fringe

Fringe guide

The second method is worked by couching down the fringe at one edge using a straight running stitch. A wide variety of threads can be used, from very fine to a thick rug wool. As there is no restriction with the stitch width a longer length fringe can be achieved. A guide is needed for length regulation; this could be a knitting needle for a short fringe or a piece of cardboard for the longer fringe.

Long fringe

Use the same colour for the stitching thread as for the fringe. If a fine thread is to be used for the fringe, double this up in multiples of very long lengths for a productive output. To keep the stitch line straight have a guide line to work to, such as a traced or tacked line marking the top edge of the fringe. Place the line mark on the fabric underneath the needle with the fringe section to the right. Using the straight running stitch fasten on and place the needle down in the fabric. Then lay the fringe threads horizontally with the short end to the left, 2cm ($\frac{3}{4}$in) over the stitch line. Secure these threads with the running stitch to the fabric on the marked line and leave the needle down in the fabric at the edge of the stitched threads. Take the long fringe thread end and wrap this around the fringe length guide to the right, then back to the left and over the marked line to lie flat. Then push these firmly up tight to the previous couched threads. Secure the fringe with the running stitch to the fabric on the marked line and leave the needle down in the fabric. (Figure 62). Complete the fringe by repeating this process. As the fringe is wrapped around the guide and

Figure 62 Long fringe. Use the fringe length guide to keep the long fringe even, push the wrapped threads up tight to the previous wrap round and couch down with a running stitch

secured to the fabric this guide will become full. Therefore release the first loops that have been secured, by pulling the guide forward to allow for further wrapping. The fringe can be left with the loops or have a cut lower edge. The top edge could also have the addition of small loops or could be embroidered with a satin stitch worked over or near the top edge.

Madeira 'Eyelet' Work

The machine must have the Madeira attachments for this and a machine fitter will make sure they are fitted correctly. The attachments are: the foot, shaft and lever, needle bar throw spindle, spur plate and pressure foot. The spur plate and pressure foot are available in sizes $\frac{7}{64}$in, $\frac{5}{32}$in, $\frac{3}{16}$in, and $\frac{1}{4}$in for the small to large eyelets.

Place the back punch in the left-hand side position, then adjust the needle width with the fitted throw spindle lock nut. This will keep the width the same throughout the work when pressure is added to the knee bar. The fabric must be held taut, with the straight grains lying correctly in a round embroidery frame. Use a punch or a stiletto to make a central hole in the fabric for the spur.

Raise the pressure foot with the left hand and pass the frame between the pressure foot and the spur plate with the right hand. Enter the spur in the hole that has been made and lower the pressure foot. Bring the underneath thread up and fasten on as for flat embroidery. Add pressure to the knee bar for the width, while turning the frame anti-clockwise. To produce the eyelet a few revolutions can be made turning the frame fairly quickly, or a single, slower turn. Release the knee bar pressure and work a few straight stitches to finish off the eyelet. Practise a few eyelets to establish a co-ordination with the most suitable working method. (Figure 63).

Figure 63 Madeira 'Eyelet' work. The fabric is held taut in a round frame and worked with the spur plate fitted to the machine

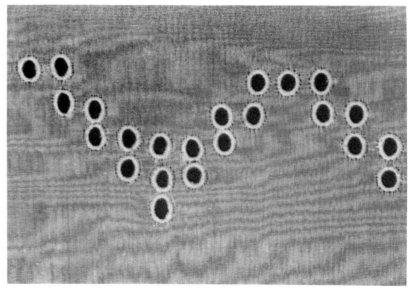

26. Care and Maintenance

These machines do create a certain amount of fluff with continuous use. The fluff must therefore be removed before it becomes compacted as this will hinder the free-working of the movements.

Remove the metal plate in the machine bed with the needle in its highest position and unscrew the two holding screws in the centre section of the three-part plate. If the machine is fitted with the one piece plate, lift this upwards and place it to one side. Clean and oil the underneath cogs and make sure there are no threads around any of the revolving parts. To the left of the cogs there is a square machine housing with a central hole; this hole should have a piece of absorbent wool inside. Drop some oil on this wool as this will lubricate the revolving shaft in the housing. Replace the metal plate back in the machine bed.

Take the top front end cover off by unscrewing the top holding nut, remove all the fluff from the needle bar and oil all the moving sections. The other oiling points are usually marked on the outer casing of the machine. However, if they are not marked, oil the top wheel and pull the top movable plate forward inside the machine housing; oil either side of the canvas drive belt. There are two oiling points further along the top of the machine above the tension disc. On the facing front plate oil the revolving shaft. On the lower edge of the support arm there is one oil point on the inside and another on the front.

At the back of the machine oil the numbered width slide plate plus the adjoining bearing pins on the link arm. Between the machine housing and the punch support there is a slanting oil point; this feeds the oil onto the cogs inside the housing. Thread the machine and give a good work through on an old piece of fabric before working on a final piece of fabric.

Domestic Machines

27. Domestic Machines

The domestic machine can be used for free embroidery and most of the techniques used on the Singer Irish. However, there is a restriction on the stitch width; most domestic machines will only work to 5cm ($\frac{3}{16}$in) width. The movement of the stitch width while working is a little difficult because the alteration must be made by hand, and not by the knee bar as with the Irish. This necessitates taking one hand away from the movement position to alter the required width regulator. If the continuous movement (see Varying Shapes: II in Chapter 22) is used the stitch width will have a degree of movement. This is when the stitch width is left in one position and the fabric is moved with a sideways movement to produce a narrow stitch, straight backwards or forwards for a wide stitch.

Leather or Suede

The advantage of the domestic machine is that of stitching leather or suede with the movement of the feed teeth and the pressure foot mechanism. A roller foot fitted to the machine will aid the movement of the leather and suede as it passes through between the roller foot and the teeth action. The rollers revolve on the surface of the leather and do not build up any friction. However, it is advisable not to work a close satin stitch on the leather or suede without a backing, as the close satin stitches will split the leathers very easily. (Figure 64).

It is possible to work decorative stitching, appliqué with a wide satin stitch, English, Italian or trapunto quilting, wool and metal thread. The other advantage the domestic machine has is in the use of the twin needles for decorative and two-colour stitching.

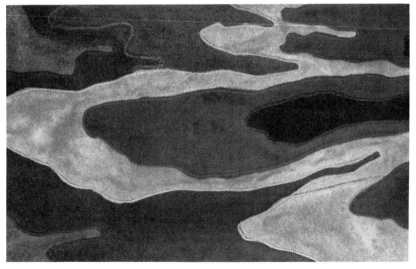

Figure 64 Leather and suede applied with the use of the roller pressure foot while using a zigzag stitch setting on the machine

28.　Free Embroidery

Adjusting the Machine

Most of the machines today have a drop feed mechanism, or a cover can be obtained to go over the teeth so that they do not come into contact with the fabric. Remove the pressure foot from the machine. Even though the pressure foot has been removed, the pressure foot lever must always be placed in its down position while working. If the lever is left up the top tension will be inoperative and the top thread will tangle underneath the work. The thread could also get tangled in the underneath race. If this is the case, make sure every thread has been removed from the underneath before resuming any stitching and make sure the foot lever is down thereafter. (Figure 65).

Fabric

Figure 65 The tucks and satin stitch are worked using the pressure foot on the machine. After the tucks have been stitched down the background areas can be decorated using a running stitch with the feed action out of use

The domestic machine needs the fabric to be held very taut, therefore it may be better to work with the fabric in the round embroidery frame. The grain must be kept absolutely straight to avoid any distortion of the fabric while it is being embroidered. If using a large frame there could be a certain amount of movement as the needle moves, and the fabric may whip up and down, in which case it would be far better to position the hands as for the Singer Irish and hold the fabric down onto the machine

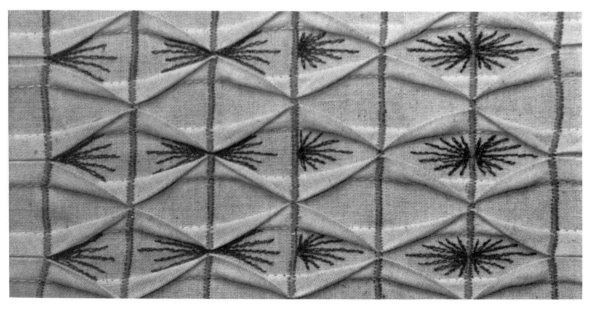

bed inside the frame. The usual habit is to hold the frame and make the movements from this outer edge; however, this is not always successful. To avoid slip stitches the fabric must be taut and must be held down onto the machine bed.

Tensions

The different machines will need slightly different adjustments, as some have bobbin cases and some have a drop-in bobbin. However, all of them should have a tension adjustment screw and, providing the tensions are adjusted to suit the particular embroidery being worked, there should not be any difficulty. While using a satin stitch the underneath thread should cover two-thirds of the width, so adjustments to the tension can be made to accomplish this. If using the metal thread, wool, cable stitch or the whip stitch, make the adjustments to the top and the underneath tensions as for the Singer Irish.

Techniques

All the techniques mentioned for the Singer Irish are possible on the domestic machine without any difficulty if the same sequence is worked. When working padded satin remember to keep to a finer wool or cord, so that the stitch width of the machine will cover the padding completely. Appliqué should be quite straightforward, as all the fabrics are applied to the ground fabric from the wrong side first. The fabric will then need only one turn and then to be reframed to complete the finishing stitches over the edge of the appliqué. All the cut work techniques can be embroidered

Figure 66 Tucks with braid. The tucks are worked first, then the lacet braid stitched down. All worked with the pressure foot and a normal straight stitch setting on the machine

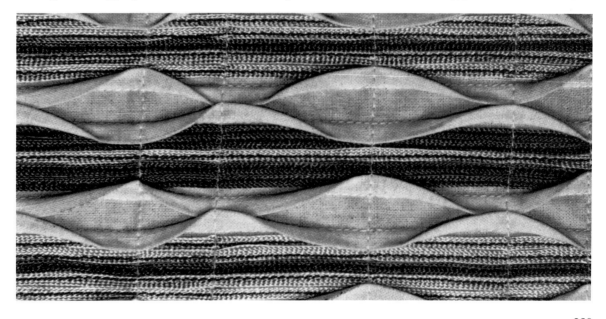

in the same way as previously explained. For the Madeira eyelets the majority of domestic machine manufacturers do produce the parts for working this method and they are easy to fit. However, the eyelets can be embroidered very successfully with the turning or the shaped method previously explained if the parts are not easily accessible. Shadow work is also straightforward, and turning the fabric in the frame is not necessary as the design is traced onto the right side of the fabric. There will be no need to use the frame when working the fringe provided the fabric is held firmly onto the machine bed while stitching. The narrow fine fringe can be worked with the foot on the machine for the straight design lines. The longer fringe is worked with the hand holding position, as the frame may prove to be a hindrance when working with a fringe guide. For evenweave fabrics the process is the same as previously explained; remove any threads before framing the fabric. Using the domestic machine for decorative embroidery will be using it to its full capacity and will enhance many articles. (Figure 66).

Tambour Embroidery

29. Tambour Embroidery

Tambour is a hand embroidery technique which is produced by holding the fabric taut in a slate frame and using a small hook needle to make a basic chain stitch, straight or in different directions.

Tambour beading is the same technique, but with every chain stitch worked a bead, sequin or bugle is sewn onto the fabric. These are sewn onto the underneath of the fabric while it is in the frame.

For both of these the technique is virtually the same. The tambour hook is held in one hand on the top of the frame, the other hand is underneath to feed the thread (and beads, if being used) onto the hook needle. Many years ago it was stipulated that the right hand must always be on the top of the frame moving the needle. However, times do change, and if a person has more self confidence using the left hand this should not prove to be any difficulty. The tambour hook is moved in certain directions to accomplish the different directional stitches. This seems a very slow process when beginning, but with practice and patience a good speed can easily be achieved with very pleasing results. The same technique has been and is being used by many embroidery firms today.

The frame size must be large enough in length – that is, the length of the webbing on the poles – to take the length of the fabric that is being embroidered. If the chain stitch is to form the embroidery, the right side of the fabric should be placed to the top in the frame. For tambour beading the right side of the fabric should be placed to the underneath when sewn into the frame.

The versatility of this technique, once it has been mastered, is endless. There are many examples explained for the initial methods, and these can be expanded with the use of different fabrics, leather and different thread materials to produce some extremely interesting embroidery.

The Slate Frame

The slate frame consists of four pieces: two round poles, with webbing nailed firmly in place from one end slot to the other end slot, and in these slots the two remaining sections, the laths. These have holes drilled along their length that are used to stretch the fabric. The other requirements are four split pins or nails, 2.5cm (1in) tape for the strapping, and straight dressmaking pins. The frame must be supported by some means at both ends; two trestles are ideal for this. These should be at a comfortable height when sitting down so as not to cause backache while working at the frame. (Figure 67). If two tables are used place pads underneath the split pins as the pins could easily mark the surface of the tables.

Figure 67 Slate frame
dressed, with the grain of the
fabric straight. The frame is
resting on two trestles, and
the two poles run
horizontally in the photo
either side of the fabric. Two
laths join the ends of the
poles. (Note the nails in each
of the four corners). The
strapping can be seen on the
left- and right-hand sides

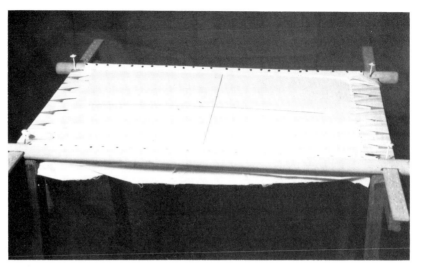

Dressing the Frame

When starting tambour work it has been found easier to use a see-through
fabric such as organdie in the frame. Some people do prefer a net as it can
guide an even stitch; however, the holes in the net could prove annoying
initially. At first it is a help to be able to see the needle and the hand with
the thread through the fabric, as it is incorrect to keep looking underneath
the frame.

Straight Grain

The fabric is ideal if it is the same length as the webbing on the poles – it
could be a little shorter, but never longer, and never wider than 45cm
(18in) wide. It is very important to have the grain of the fabric absolutely
straight in the frame to avoid distorting the fabric. Move the free edges of
the webbing facing each other, place the laths through the end slots of
both the poles and then set the frame square.

Sewing into frame

Turn over 1cm ($\frac{1}{2}$in) along the edges of the fabric; pin the centre of the
length of fabric to the centre of the webbing on both of the poles. Slightly
stretch each of the four corners with the turned over edge of the fabric and
pin these to the relevant four corners on the webbing. Thus, having each
length of the fabric turned over and pinned to the webbing, sew this edge
to the webbing with 1cm ($\frac{1}{2}$in) stitches. The fabric is stretched out by
placing the split pins to the inside of the poles into the holes of the laths;
the distance between the poles must be equal on both sides. (Figure 67).

Strapping

To tighten the width of the fabric the tape is pinned to the edge and taken round the laths. Start on the left side and pin a length of tape flat along the side edge of the fabric; then, at right angles to this and through both thicknesses, pin the tape for strapping. (Figure 67). Take the strapping over and under the lath, pull a little and pin onto the two thicknesses of the width next to the previous strapping. Then take the strapping under and over the lath, pull the width just a little and onto the two thicknesses, again next to the previous strapping. Continue in this manner; the next strapping will go over and under the lath; pull the width a little, and pin through the two thicknesses. This alternate over and under, under and over will allow the strapping to fall easily from the laths when reframing.

While strapping this first side do remember the straight grain of the fabric; this first side should not be pulled too tight and so make the grain form a curve. After the first side has been strapped the second side is strapped in the same way. Either turn the frame around or stand the other side, then it can be strapped from the left again. The frame can be tightened a little after the strapping has been completed. Pull the pole back a little and reposition the split pins; this must be stretched both ends of the pole to keep the distance of each lath equal.

A Long Fabric

If a very long piece of fabric is to be embroidered, sew the length onto the webbing as previously described and then release the front pole from the laths. Then take another piece of fabric; this is for rolling in and will be loose, not stitched to the frame. Lay this second piece of fabric over the frame and take one edge to the underneath of the nearest pole to lie smooth and go underneath the webbing. Then give this pole a few turns under so that both the fabrics are rolled around the pole and the loose fabric is being held in place. Now bring the loose fabric from the top of the frame over the pole to hang down from the underneath. The rolling in can be continued until a working width is reached. In doing this both the framed fabric and the loose fabric must be kept absolutely smooth along the length of the pole. If creases are rolled in these will be difficult to remove, and the frame will be difficult to tighten evenly. The rolling in will pull out a little when the frame is stretched, so when the working width is reached given one or two more turns under with the pole. Place the laths back in the pole ends; stretch the frame and strap as before.

After the first working width has been embroidered, reframing will be necessary. First roll out the next required section, then roll in the embroidered section as follows: take the split pins out and release the strapping by taking the pins out, release the laths from the rolled in pole and roll out the second working width. Place the laths back in the first pole and release the laths from the second pole; this way the strapping remains on the laths. Use a second piece of loose fabric to roll in the completed embroidery width of fabric; again both fabrics must be smooth. Place the laths back in the second pole, stretch and strap for the second working width. Complete the long piece of embroidery this way by rolling out and rolling in.

Small Fabric

If quite a few small pieces of fabric are to be embroidered these can be framed in two different ways. Firstly, if all the small pieces are the same size they can be tacked together to form a strip or square not longer than the pole; this is framed as previously described.

Secondly, if the small pieces are all different sizes, dress the frame with a piece of close woven cotton fabric such as calico. Place the small pieces that are to be embroidered on the top of the dressed frame and treat these in the same manner as for framing. Pin the top edge of the piece in the centre to the dressed frame fabric and slightly stretch each corner out; pin these, then pin the fabric in between. The pins should be fairly close together if these pieces are not going to be tacked in place. Now pull the centre of the lower edge towards the pole and pin. Slightly stretch each lower corner down and outwards, keeping the lower line straight, with the centre lower edge and these corners directly under the top corners. Then pin in position. Pin in between these three pins of the lower line to make secure. Now pin the sides in this manner, centres first; slightly stretch and pin in position. (Figure 68).

Turn the frame over and pull the close woven fabric up and away from the small piece that has just been pinned in. Cut this back fabric along the lower line and up the two sides, inside the pin lines. Fold the fourth side back and pin it onto the frame fabric. Turn the frame back and complete the embroidery on the small piece of fabric. There could easily be more than one small piece put in the frame in this way, in which case complete all the embroidery on the pieces and then remove them from the frame. When these have been taken out of the frame, all the sections of cut fabric can be oversewn back together for the framing of more small pieces of fabric.

Figure 68 Small pieces of fabric slightly stretched and pinned onto the frame fabric with the grain of these pieces straight

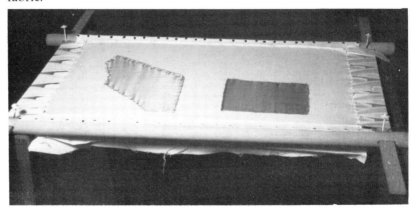

30. Tambour Holder

The tambour holder is usually made from wood, either shaped with a think centre section or in a straight pencil shape. The holder section has a metal end with a needle hole at the base. This section has a thumb screw through the metal to hold the needle in place. (Figure 69).

Front of Holder

The thumb screw is at the front of the holder and the front hook of the needle must be positioned beneath this thumb screw. The needle has a smooth back leading to the smooth back of the holder. The length of the needle can vary from 8mm to 12mm (about $\frac{3}{8}$–$\frac{1}{2}$in). This working length is entirely individual for each person; some prefer a short needle while others a long one. (Figure 69).

Figure 69 The wooden, shaped tambour holder

Figure 70 The tambour holder must always be held straight up in a vertical position for the easy movement of the hook in and out of the fabric

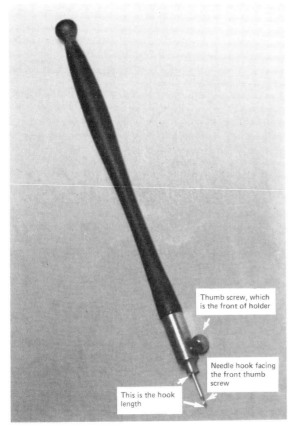

Thumb screw, which is the front of holder

Needle hook facing the front thumb screw

This is the hook length

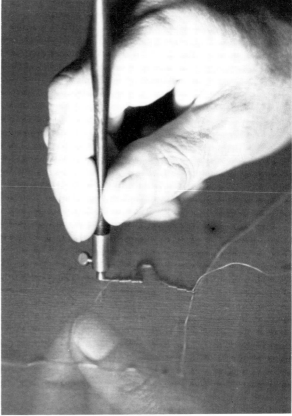

Correct Holding

The tambour holder must always be held straight up in a vertical position, never on the slant like a pencil or pen. This is because when the needle is used in a straight position it is less likely to pull the threads or make a hole in the fabric. If it is ever held slanting the needle will continually catch the threads of the fabric and working the tambour stitches will be extremely exhausting. The thumb screw should always face the direction that is being worked. (Figure 70).

Needle Sizes

The needle sizes are exactly the same as for the Cornely hook sizes. These needles are broken near the thick section and the hook is used for tambour. The small sizes are for a fine thread and the large sizes for a thicker thread or wool. Use the short or medium hook length size for tambour as the length of the long hook could prove cumbersome.

31. Fastening On

All the instructions that follow are for right-handed people; reverse all the instructions if you are left handed. Use a spool of thread and support this with a long nail or knitting needle; put this through the spool and then through a hole in the lath. Hold the thread between the thumb and forefinger of the left hand, with the thread to the spool between the third and small finger and the short end over the back of the hand. The left hand is underneath the frame while working. Rest the right arm on the pole of the frame, hold the tambour holder vertically in the right hand with the front thumb screw facing left; this is for working to the left.

1. Put the needle down into the fabric.

2. Loop the underneath thread over the hook needle with the thumb and forefinger. Diagram 38 (1).

3. Turn the hook or thumb screw to the back or facing right. 38 (2).

4. Push a little pressure onto the smooth back of the needle or push to the left.

5. Bring the needle up to the top of the fabric while keeping the slight pushing pressure to the left; the needle must have the thread in the hook. 38 (3).

6. Turn the thumb screw to face the left while keeping the thread on the hook. 38 (4).

7. Put the needle down into the fabric with the thumb screw facing left, a little further to the left of the insertion position at stage 1, to make a small stitch.

8. Loop the shorter end of the underneath thread over the hook needle with the thumb and forefinger.

9. Turn the thumb screw to the back or facing right. 38 (5).

10. Push a little pressure onto the smooth back of the needle; push to the left.

11. Bring the needle up to the top of the fabric while keeping the slight pressure to the left and the thread in the hook.

12. Bring this short end of thread to the top of the fabric. 38 (6).

Secure Fastening On

13. Put the needle down into the fabric with the thumb screw facing left a fraction in front of the previous stitch.

14. Loop the underneath thread over the hook with the thumb and forefinger. 38 (7).

15. Turn the thumb screw to the back facing right.

16. Push a little pressure onto the smooth back of the hook and bring the needle up to the top of the fabric with the thread in the hook.

17. Keep the thumb screw facing right and then put the needle down at the beginning of the first stitch made as for No. 1.

18. Loop the underneath thread over the hook with the thumb and forefinger. 38 (8).

19. Turn the thumb screw to the left, push a little pressure onto the smooth back of the needle and bring it up to the top of the fabric with the thread in the hook. 38 (9).

All these movements explained for the fastening on and securing the fastening on complete the initial movements that are essential for holding the beginning secure. These initial chain stitches should be no bigger than 1.5mm (about $\frac{1}{16}$in), after which the chain stitch can be worked.

Chain Stitch

Continue working to the left and produce a straight line.

20. Face the thumb screw to the left and put it down through the fabric at the end of the fastening on stitches at No. 19.

Fastening on

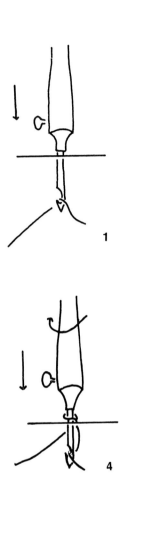

1

2

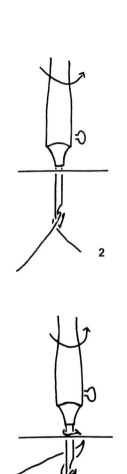

3

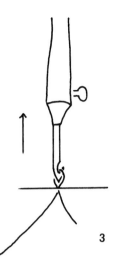

4

5

6

7

8

9

21. Loop the underneath thread over the hook with the thumb and forefinger.

22. Turn the thumb screw to the right, add slight pressure to the smooth back of the needle and bring it to the top of the fabric with the thread in the hook. One chain stitch as in Figure 71.

23. Turn the thumb screw to the left and put the needle down through the fabric a little further to the left, making a small stitch.

24. As No. 21, loop the underneath thread over the hook with the thumb and forefinger.

25. As No. 22.

26. As No. 23.

These movements 20 to 22 construct one chain stitch. (Figure 71).

Continue these movements along the line from right to left until competent then turn and work in different directions. Up, down in a vertical direction and then fill in a shape starting on the outside. Keep the distance between each line equal for each line.

The thread should not be held too tight in the left hand because this will easily give a very tight stitch and pull the fabric into gathers.

Diagram 38 Fastening on
1. 1 & 2 Needle down with the thread hooked over the needle
2. 3 Needle turned to the back while holding the thread
3. 4 & 5 Add slight pressure to the back of the needle while bringing the thread to the top
4. 7 & 8 Needle down for a short stitch with the short end of thread looped over the needle
5. 9 Needle turned to the back while holding the short end of thread
6. 10, 11, 12 Add pressure to the back of the needle while bringing the short end of thread to the top
7. 13 & 14 Needle down with the thread looped over the needle
8. 15, 16, 17 & 18 The needle has been brought to the top of the fabric, put down again to the right and the thread looped over the needle
9. 19 Needle turned and brought up to the top of fabric while holding the loop of thread for commencement of work

Fastening Off

This is a little more complex than the fastening on; the loop is knotted twice with the previous loop. These are worked by going back a fraction by the side of the previous chain line, not by going forward for each knot. (Diagram 39).

1. Pull the last loop of thread a little longer in length, then go back just a fraction and pull a loop of thread through the first by making the movements as for the chain stitch. Diagram 39 (1).

2. Slip the needle through the second loop of thread and catch the first loop with the hook needle. 39 (2).

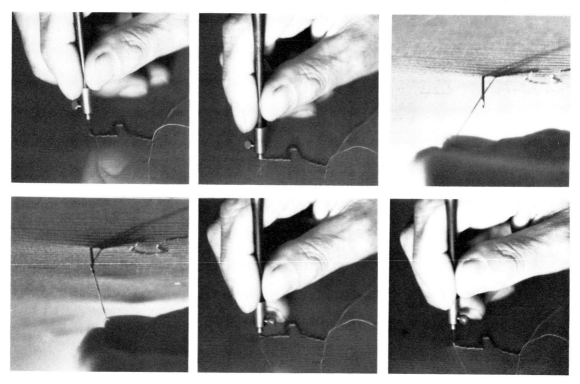

Figure 71 Fastening on. The movements for working one complete chain stitch

3. Pull the thread down with the left hand underneath; this will tighten the second loop around the first loop on the needle for the first knot. 39 (3).

4. Pull another loop through the fabric and the first loop, slip the needle through this third loop of thread and catch the first loop again with the hook needle. 39 (4), (5), (6).

5. Pull the thread down with the left hand underneath; as before, it will tighten on the first loop and this will form the second knot. 39 (7). After the second knot bring the thread through the fabric again and cut the last loop of thread to fasten off. 39 (8), (9).

Diagram 39 Fastening off
1. 1 Pull the thread up to make a little longer loop
2. 2 Slip the needle through the second loop and catch the first loop on the hook of the needle
3. 3 Pull the thread down tight underneath for the first knot
4. 4 Needle down with the thread looped over the needle and turned
5. 4 Needle up with the thread to make a little longer loop
6. 4 Slip the needle through the loop and catch the previous loop on the hook of the needle
7. 5 Pull the thread down tight underneath for the second knot
8. 5 Needle down with the thread looped on the needle
9. 5 Needle up with the loop of thread which is cut; pull unwanted thread down

Fastening off

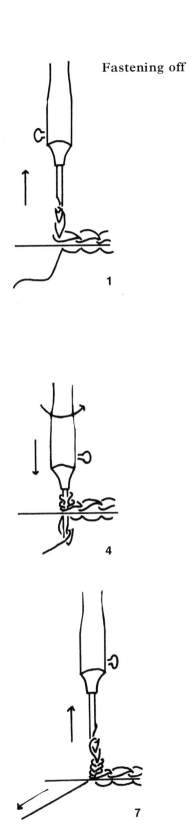

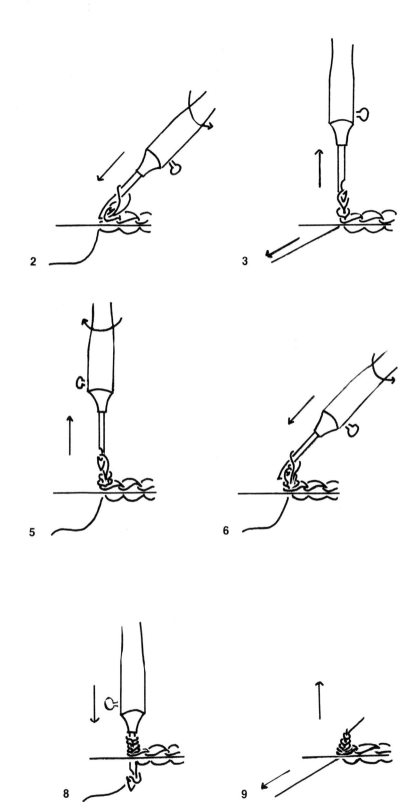

1

2

3

4

5

6

7

8

9

32. Movement

After proficiency has been achieved with the previous fasten on, chain stitch and fasten off, proceed with the movement. The chain stitch can easily be worked with movement to give a different appearance; these techniques can also be used to produce some very interesting results.

Zigzag

Diagram 40 Movement. Chain stitch used for a zigzag movement

The chain stitch is continually worked this time with a zigzag movement. The length of the stitch can vary as this will depend on what it is required for. It can be a zigzag with a triangle shape, or it can be worked very close together to give almost a satin stitch, having a centre interest.

For the triangle zigzag have two tack lines, one for the top stitch line, the other for the lower stitch line. Fasten on with small diagonal stitches and cover this with the first diagonal stitch to the top line. Then make a diagonal stitch to the lower tack line. Keep the distance between each stitch on both lines equal throughout. Continue with the diagonal stitches for the distance required to achieve the necessary ease of movement. (Diagram 40).

If a long diagonal stitch is required the stitch will slip back from the point. This may be desired for an interesting effect as it gives a centre zigzag with a straight stitch coming from the points. If, however, this is not required, work a very small chain stitch at the very end of each point of the diagonal stitches. These directional stitches should make a diagonal stitch to the top tack line; then make a very small horizontal stitch, make a diagonal stitch to the lower tack line and then a very small horizontal stitch. This will hold the diagonal stitches in place without the slip back.

Pulled zigzag

Work two tack lines marking the top and lower stitch lines. Fasten on with a very small vertical stitch and cover this with the first vertical stitch to the top tack line. Hold the underneath thread a little tight and draw back this last stitch in a downward direction until the first loop is in the centre of the two tack lines. Release the hold on the underneath thread as the needle is taken down for the next stitch on the lower tack line, almost next to the previous stitch. Hold the underneath thread a little tight and draw the last stitch back in an upwards direction until the second loop is in the centre of the two tack lines. Release the hold on the underneath thread as the needle is taken up for the next stitch on the top tack line almost next to the previous stitch. This will give the appearance of a small zigzag in the centre of a simulated satin stitch. (Figure 72).

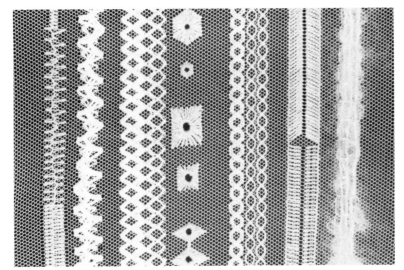

Figure 72 (From left to right). The first two examples are varieties of pulled zigzag used to give a centre interest, then small stitches used to form a zigzag, drawback pulled into the centre to form a centre hole, small stitches used to form a wave, drawback diagonal and straight and drawback used for couching a mohair wool

It is not absolutely necessary to have the small zigzag in the centre of the satin stitch. If required it can be made to move within the length of the simulated satin stitch. This is regulated by the amount of tension put on the underneath thread as it is held for the drawn back movement.

Draw back

The appearance of this stitch resembles that of buttonhole stitch when it is worked close together. It has a small chain stitch at the lower edge of the vertical stitches. This can easily be used for cut-out work, the cut edge being the lower small chain stitch.

Make the two tack or design lines the required width apart for the top and lower edges. Fasten on with small stitches along the lower line.

1. Take a stitch vertically up to the top line.

2. Hold the underneath thread a little tight and draw the needle with the thread back to the lower line.

3. Take a stitch in the same place as the first stitch right at the lower end of this vertical stitch.

4. Now make a small horizontal stitch along the lower line.

5. Take a stitch vertically up to the top line.

6. Hold the underneath thread a little tight and draw the needle with the thread back to the lower line.

7. Take a stitch in the same place as the fifth stitch right at the lower end of this vertical stitch.

8. Make a small horizontal stitch along the lower line. (Diagram 41).

These movements make two draw back stitches. Continue with these four movements to formulate one stitch until the desired length has been reached.

Diagram 41 Chain stitch used for a drawback movement

33.   Fabric

Almost any fabric can be used for tambour. However, if using a fabric that has a great deal of stretch it may not recover its original size if it is left in the frame for any length of time.

Net

Tambour on net is governed to a certain extent by the mesh of the net, i.e. whether one works one stitch to each hole or one stitch to two holes of the mesh. Many interesting directional movements can be made and the varied filling stitches can be used, as in Coggeshall lace; this was the use of chain stitches worked on net, in the late nineteenth and early twentieth century. Different thicknesses of thread are easily used on the net and add interest as well as dimension. Thread the same colour as the net and different colours can be used; if using black on black it would be much better for the eyes to work this in natural daylight in order not to get eye strain.

For this embroidery the net is sewn in the frame and the right side will be the topside. Sew a strip of material or tape along the four sides of the net before sewing into the frame to stop the net splitting on the pins.

The design can be tacked in position on the net or drawn on with a pencil that is not too soft. Place the design underneath the net, then tack or draw this in position. As this method is worked from the right side all the ends of thread are taken to the back and fastened off in the back of the stitching.

Chain stitch, zigzag and draw back stitch can be used on the net, as well as appliqué and cut-out techniques. The appliqué could utilize other nets in different quantities or single layers of fabric such as organza, dress silk or a satin. Two layers of net could be stitched together and have a padding threaded through between the stitch lines. (Figures 73 and 74).

Cut-out

The cut-out technique can be used on most of the close woven fabrics; organza, silk, rayon and wool are only a few. This method is achieved by using the chain stitch and the draw back stitch. The cut-out sections should be fairly small to avoid distortion.

Trace the design onto the right side of the fabric and frame this with the right side to the top. Work a straight chain line around the cut-out shape with a medium tension; if it is too loose it will not hold the shape. Then work over the chain stitch to cover it completely with the draw back stitches, keeping the small horizontal stitch to the cut-out edge. The

Figure 73 Different
thicknesses of thread in
shades of one colour
Figure 74 The lower edges
of the appliqué are worked
first with a straight chain line
covered with a small zigzag.
These shapes are applied
with a small zigzag stitch

depth of the draw back will vary as to the design requirements. As this method is worked from the right side take all the ends of thread to the back and fasten them off through the back of the stitching. Finish all the embroidery and take the work out of the frame. Use a sharp pair of scissors and cut out the sections carefully, close to the horizontal stitches. Then give a final press with the right side of the work down onto a soft pad. (Figure 75).

Figure 75 Cut out. (Left) The shapes have a straight chain line covered with a drawback stitch pulled into the open centre. Appliqué. (Right) The top loose shapes have a zigzag edge, the lower larger shapes have a drawback edge

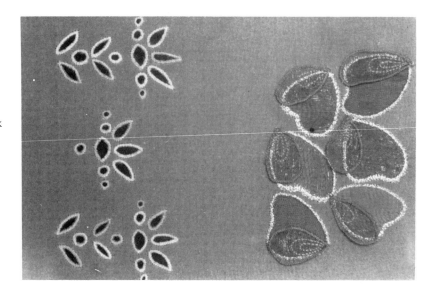

Appliqué

This technique can be worked on organza, silk, satin, rayon and wool, using the stitches described. There are two working methods that can be used, depending on the fabric and the design.

If a see-through organza fabric is being used the design is traced onto the right side. The fabric is framed with the right side up. Lay the organza appliqué over the design to make sure the lines can be seen through clearly. The appliqué fabric must be large enough to cover the design, plus a little extra for pinning.

After the background fabric has been framed, place the appliqué piece over the section that is to have the appliqué work. The straight grain must be in the same direction on both the background and the appliqué fabric. Pin the appliqué piece in position; preferably, pin on a design line to avoid marking the background. It is important to stretch the appliqué piece slightly in both directions to avoid this showing a bobble effect when the work is removed from the frame. If the design cannot be seen through the appliqué, trace these sections onto the appliqué piece, remembering the straight grain direction. The appliqué is pinned in the same way as before; however, this time the top design must be placed exactly on top of the ground fabric design and all the lines must match as it is pinned in position.

Outline the design with two lines of chain stitch worked very close together. Over the two chain lines stitch a very small zigzag; the width should only be the width of the two chain lines. (Figure 75). After this section has been completed, use a sharp pair of scissors to cut away the surplus outside fabric. Apply all the fabrics in this way and complete all the embroidery before removing the ground fabric from the frame.

If using a fabric that cannot be seen through for the design, the double tracing method can be used, as explained above. The second technique is to trace the design onto the wrong side of the ground fabric. Frame the ground fabric with the right side to the top. On this right side pin the appliqué fabric, remembering to give this a slight stretch. Turn the frame over to work from the wrong side and stitch one chain line around the design line of the appliqué section. Turn the frame back to the right side and stitch the second chain line by the side of the straight stitch line of the first chain line. Over these two chain lines stitch a very small zigzag or a draw back stitch, which could have some width if this is desired. Use a sharp pair of scissors to cut away the surplus outside fabric close to the stitch line. (Figure 75). The latter method will require the frame to be turned over for each appliqué piece; however, this should not prove to be too difficult. Complete all the embroidery before removing from the frame.

If using leather for the appliqué, stitch one straight chain line around the design and cut away the surplus outside leather. After this the edge of the leather can be stitched over with a zigzag or a draw back stitch, going through the stitch holes of the first line to give a neater finish.

Padding

Double fabric is used for this technique; either a see-through organza or a solid fabric can be used, depending on the desired effect. If using organza a coloured wool is threaded through from the back between the two layers of fabric for the padding, so that the direction lines of the padding will show through. If using a solid fabric, a wool or padding can be threaded through from the back between the two layers; this will not show the direction lines.

The two layers of fabric are framed together; if working a very large piece then it would be advantageous to cross tack together through the centre. The right or wrong side tracing will depend on the desired effect. If the chain stitch is required to show on the right side then trace on this side and frame with the right side to the top. If a straight stitch is required to show on the right side, then trace on the wrong side and frame with the wrong side to the top. There could be a mixture of both chain and straight stitches, in which case the chain stitch lines will be worked through for a guide line as in the appliqué method. Then the chain stitch can be worked on the right side.

After all the stitching has been completed, remove the tack line and leave the fabric in the frame, but make the fabric a little slack by moving

Figure 76 Padding. Chain
stitch worked from the right
and the wrong side to obtain
different stitch effects; the use
of a metal thread adds a little
sparkle

the split pins in by one or two holes on the laths. The padding is worked
from the wrong side of the work; it is necessary to turn the frame over for
this. Thread the wool through a fairly blunt needle (a tapestry needle
could be used), work through one layer of the fabric only and pad each
area evenly by working from one side to the other, with the padding side
by side. If working on organza the padding threads will show, therefore
make sure the padding threads lie side by side. As the padding is pulled
through the first line leave a little of the pad threads showing at the edge.
Leave a fraction of fabric by the side of this first line and enter the wool
again for the second padding threads to lie by the side of the first line. Pull
the second line through and leave a very small loop at the edge. This must
never be pulled tight; always allow for the wool stretching as most wools
have elastic qualities. (Figure 76). Pad all the areas and then remove the
fabric from the frame. If required, steam the fabric while holding it in its
shape; never put a heavy dry iron onto padding as it will only press in
creases.

34. Tambour Beading

Beads

In the purchase of beads, bugles and sequins, always endeavour to buy them ready strung on a length of thread; if they are not, then they must be threaded. Beads vary in size, which will necessitate varying the chain stitch size. The design is traced on the wrong side of the fabric and framed with the wrong side to the top. Do remember to reverse an asymmetric design before tracing so that it is the right way round when completed. Choose a thread to match the beads or the fabric. (A fine metal thread could also be used). If a colour is used the thread will add colour when using clear crystal beads. If required, beads could be used on the previous techniques with the cut-out, appliqué and padding.

Threading

For threading the beads onto the spool thread, keep the beads on top of the frame in case they spill; they will then be easier to re-thread, and you won't have to pick them up from the floor. Use one end of thread from the threaded beads to make a loose knot. Take this thread around the forefinger, cross the thread over to form a circle and slip the short end through the circle to form a loose knot. Now take the end of thread from the spool and pass this through the circle of the loose knot for 10cm (4in) as though threading a needle. (Diagram 42). Pull the loose knot tight around the spool thread. After this is secure, pass the beads over onto the spool thread a few at a time, in case the thread snaps in two, until all the beads have been passed over onto the spool thread.

 The second technique, and one used in the industry, could be considered a little quicker. However, more care is needed in order to avoid spilling all the beads on the floor. Again, keep the beads on the top of the frame. Hold one end of the thread from the threaded beads over the

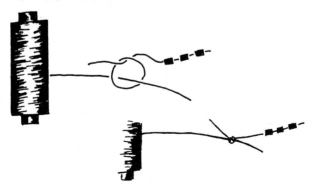

Diagram 42 When threading the beads onto the spool thread, the loose knot is always made with the thread holding the beads. The spool thread is passed through the bead loop as though threading the eye of a needle

forefinger of the left hand. Hold the tambour hook in the right hand; with the hook split the bead thread on the forefinger of the left hand in two and push the hook through a little. Loop the spool thread into the hook needle, pull this back through the split thread and have 10cm (4in) of the short end of the spool thread looped through the split thread. Then pass the beads over as before, a few at a time. (Beads, bugles and sequins are passed onto the spool thread in the same way).

Beading

Fasten on and use the chain stitch; to every chain stitch a bead is worked. Have a few beads from the spool thread resting in the palm of the left hand between the thumb and forefinger and before the thread passes round the little finger.

One bead must be pushed up to be just underneath the fabric. Then, when the thread is held between the thumb and forefinger, the bead will not be able to slip down. (Figure 77). After the bead has been pushed up the thread is looped over the needle. As the needle is put down through the fabric push one bead up with the left forefinger; the thumb is used to help separate the one bead. Then loop the thread over the hook of the needle. Turn the needle; add a slight pressure to pull up and make the next stitch. This stitch must be the same length as the bead that is being used. Put the needle down, push up one bead, loop the thread onto the needle, turn the needle and pull up for the next stitch. Repeat these movements for each stitch.

These movements will easily become automatic with practice, and quite a good speed will be achieved.

Figure 77 Tambour beading. As the needle is put down through the fabric push one bead up with the left forefinger, hold the bead in position, then loop the thread over the hook needle

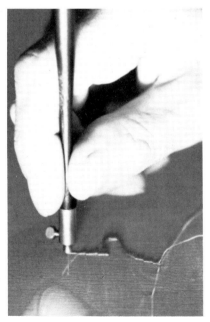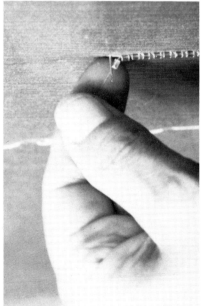

Looped Beads

This technique is worked by using the chain zigzag and the draw back stitches, as well as by pushing up a number of beads instead of one; these must lie flat on the surface of the fabric. The number of beads that are pushed up will be determined by the length of the chain zigzag or the draw back stitch; this could be six beads or more at a time. The zigzag is worked as for the chain, and the number of beads is pushed up before the thread is looped over the needle. Secure the points of the zigzag with a small stitch. The draw back stitch has the required number of beads pushed up in place as the stitch is drawn back to the lower edge. (See Draw Back section, No. 2). Put the needle down in the same place as the previous stitch, as in draw back No. 3, and make the stitch with the beads in place. Make the horizontal stitch equal in length to the width of the beads; this should give sufficient distance between the two vertical lines for the beads to lie flat on the surface of the fabric. (Figure 78). Take the vertical stitch up, draw back and push the beads up as the needle is put down at the lower end of the vertical stitch. Pull up the thread and make the horizontal stitch the width of the bead. These movements are repeated for each looped draw back stitch.

Stand Up Beads

These are a form of looped beads that are stitched to stand up instead of lying flat on the surface of the material. The beads are counted in an odd number (three, five or seven) to avoid showing the thread at the top of the loop.

Figure 78 The two groups of beads on the left are looped beads, the rest are stand-up beads. For the chain looped beads make a small chain stitch at the edge of the bead lines to accommodate the width of the bead being used. The looped beads will then lie side by side instead of producing a crossover effect. In the bottom centre of the photo, three beads are pushed up for a small stand. Different heights are achieved by pushing more odd numbers of beads

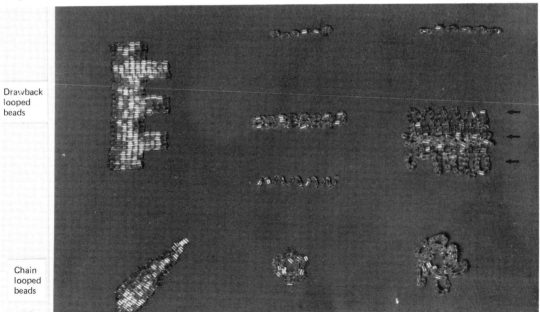

Drawback looped beads

Chain looped beads

Five bead stand

Five, seven and nine bead stands

Five, seven and nine bead stand

143

All the stitches are the same length and must be the width of the beads being used. Put the needle down for the first stitch, push up the required number of beads, then loop the thread over the needle and bring the needle up to the top. Make a stitch with the thread only. Put the needle down for the third stitch, push up the required number of beads, then loop the thread over the needle and bring the needle up to the top. Make a stitch with the thread only. Continue with one bead loop stitch and one thread only; stitch until the required length has been completed.

This method can look very effective if worked in a circle or as an outline for a solid flat bead filling. (Figure 78).

Fringe Beads

The fringe has a longer loop of beads than the stand up beads; this fringe can be 3–20cm (1–8in) or longer if required. A guide is used to keep the lengths of the fringe the same throughout. The guide is made from a piece of cardboard longer than the length of the fringe; this has two vertical pencil marks from one edge to mark the length of the fringe required. The guide is left on the top of the frame for easy measurement of the fringe. All the stitches are the same length and these must be the width of the bead when working a close fringe.

Put the needle down for the first stitch, bring the beads up and measure the required number of beads off on the guide between the two marked lines for the length of the fringe. Separate the remaining beads on the spool thread from the fringe length. (Figure 79). Push the fringe beads up to the underneath of the fabric, loop the thread from the end of the fringe onto the needle; the beads should be in between the stitch. (Figure 79). Bring the thread up and then make one stitch with the thread only. Put the needle down for the third stitch, bring the beads up to measure the second fringe loop. Separate the beads and push the fringe beads to the underneath of the fabric and loop the thread onto the needle with the beads in between the stitch. As the thread is looped over for the third

Figure 79 Fringe. (Left) Make a guide double the length of the fringe required to keep the fringe the same length throughout. (Right) Push the fringe beads to the underneath of the fabric and loop the thread over the needle

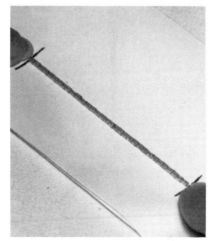

stitch care must be taken not to catch the first loop of beads with the needle. It will help to avoid any catching if the loops are pinned flat to the fabric. This is easy to do without turning the frame over: push the loop up to the fabric underneath and put the pin in from the top to go through the round end of the loop. The other method is to push the loop to one side with the forefinger of the left hand and loop the thread over with the thumb; bring the thread up and make one stitch with the thread only. Continue in this manner with one loop stitch and one thread stitch for the length required. (Figure 80).

It is possible to have a double loop which could be worked in two colours. For this make the thread-only stitch longer or work three bead width stitches instead of one. Then, when the second row of looped beads is worked, there will be sufficient room between it and the first row to accommodate the width of beads required. This will give the effect of a crossover loop; there are many variations that can be worked on this theme. (Figures 81 and 82).

Figure 80 Finished fringe

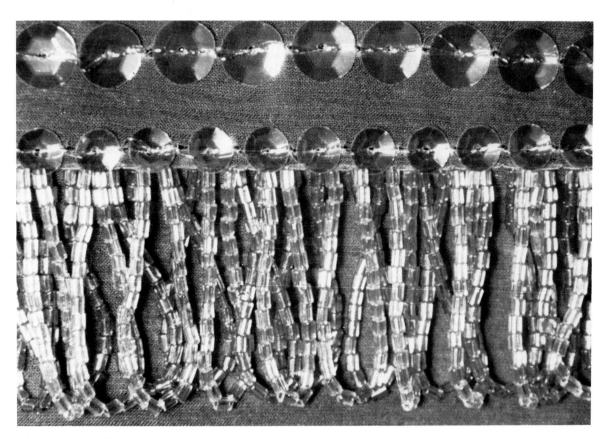

Spaced Beads

This technique involves the use of stitches in thread only worked in between the beads. It will depend on how much space is required as to

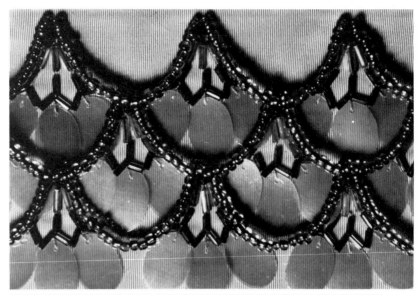

Figure 81 Loop fringe
Figure 82 For a single strand bead fringe thread the beads onto double thread. For the free hanging end, knot the two ends of thread together, open the two threads, then pull a bead down from the threaded string to go between the two opened threads. From this secured end measure the length for the hang of the fringe; leave 8cm (3in) of double thread at the top end to tambour the fringe in position

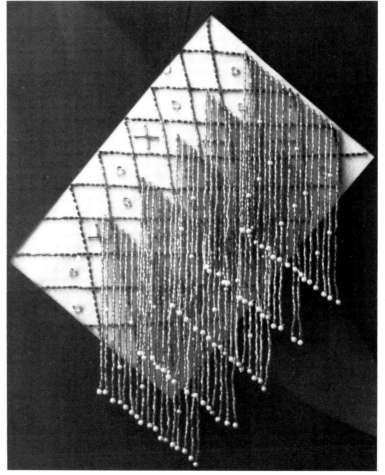

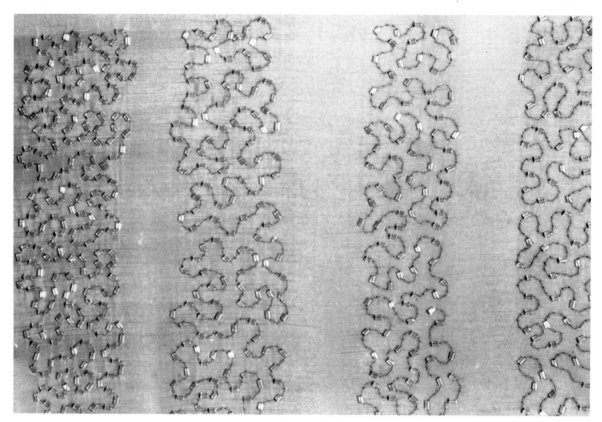

how many stitches are worked in this way. For this method the spool thread is usually the exact match to the fabric being embroidered; however, a fine metal thread is often used and gives a very pleasing result. For a close spacing work one bead and one stitch; for more spacing increase the number of thread-only stitches in between the beads. Care must be taken with this method not to make the thread-only stitches too large; keep these the same size as the beads being used. This method should also be kept looking neat, not with threads crossing over, unless it is an elaborate design for the thread-only stitches. (Figure 83).

Figure 83 Spaced beads. (From left to right) One bead and one stitch; One bead and two stitches; One bead and three stitches; One bead and four stitches

35. Bugles

Bugles are longer than the beads and they are also made in different lengths. The number of the bugle denotes the length: No. 1, No. 2, No. 3, No. 4, No. 6 and No. 15, the shortest being No. 1 ($\frac{1}{8}$in, 3mm); No. 15 is $1\frac{1}{8}$in, 3cm, long. These will need a longer stitch than that used for the beads. They can be worked in a straight line using chain zigzag stitch; however, more frequently they are used with the draw back stitch.

The chain and zigzag with the small holding stitch are worked as for the looped beads, i.e. one bugle to one stitch, that is unless looped bugles are required, in which case a number of bugles are used with a stitch length to accommodate the bugles.

Draw Back Bugles

For the draw back there is one bugle to one vertical stitch; this will make them lie side by side. The bugle is pushed up as the stitch is drawn back to the lower edge. If the bugle is pushed up as the stitch is taken to the top line two errors could happen. The first is that as the thread is drawn back it would be pulled through the bugle; as some bugles have a sharp edge the thread could easily be cut. The second is that as the thread is drawn back it could easily be crossed over; then the thread would lie diagonally over the surface of the bugle. Therefore make the vertical stitch to the top line with the thread only, then draw back to the lower edge (No. 2 of the draw back method) as the bugle is pushed up in place. Put the needle

Figure 84 Bugles. (From left to right) Chain stitch; Zigzag; Drawback (two methods)

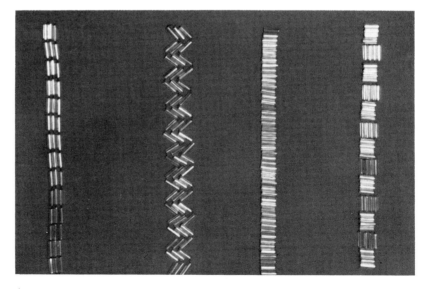

down in the same place as the previous stitch (draw back No. 3) and make the stitch which will hold the bugle in place. Make the horizontal stitch equal in length to the width of the bugle; this should give sufficient distance between the two vertical stitches for the bugle to lie flat on the surface of the fabric. After this the next vertical stitch is made to accommodate the next bugle. It is important to remember that the stitch must be long enough for the size of bugle being used, otherwise it will pull away from the fabric. However, it should never be longer, because thread showing either side of a bugle would be extremely ugly and the bugle will move along the stitch to make a very uneven line. (Figure 84).

36.   Sequins

Sequins are round with a centre hole and are made in different sizes. The number denotes the diameter of the sequin in millimetres. These are: No. 3, No. 4, No. 5, No. 6, No. 8, No. 10, No. 12 and No. 15. They are made flat or cup-shaped; the cup sequins have a flat centre with six facets on the outer raised edge. The sequins can be tamboured so that they overlap each other; this method is called scaled sequins, with one sequin to one stitch for a straight chain line or the zigzag. They can be stitched both sides to lie flat or stitched one side with the draw back.

The sequins must be threaded onto the spool thread the right way because there is a right and wrong side to the sequins. The right side is of course the shiniest, the wrong side has a very small ridge around the outer perimeter. The right side of the cup sequin is self explanatory: the outer raised edge denotes the right side. To transfer the sequins onto the spool thread, the slip knot is put in the end of the thread with the right side of the sequin facing the slip knot, or the right side of the sequin facing the spool thread.

Scaled Sequins

For tambour the size of the stitch is half the size of the sequin; this is the measurement from the centre hole to the outer edge. The scaled sequins are worked with the use of the chain stitch, pushing up one sequin to one chain stitch. This centre hole of the sequin must always be covered with the following sequin. (Figure 85). If working straight vertical lines on a garment the sequins should brush down. Therefore always start at the lower edge or hem and work up to the top. If the sequins are difficult to separate moisten the thumb and forefinger slightly; this will help to detach them and so work them singly.

Zigzag and Draw Back

The zigzag stitch is worked with one sequin to one stitch; this will give a slightly wider line than the straight chain stitch. For the draw back the vertical stitch must be half the width of the sequin, and the sequin is pushed up as the stitch is drawn back to the lower edge. The horizontal stitch must be the full width of the sequin; the centre hole will show with this method of the draw back. (Figure 85).

Flat Sequins

The flat sequin is stitched on with three stitches to one sequin. Make a thread-only stitch half the width of the sequin being used; draw this stitch back to the beginning of the stitch. Push one sequin up in place and make a stitch at the beginning of the previous stitch; this will be on the outer edge of the sequin. Now work forward; make a stitch with the thread only, going through the centre hole of the sequin and another thread-only stitch to the outer edge of the sequin. (Figure 85). These last two stitches are going forward on the stitch line. Make a thread-only stitch forward, half the width of the sequin, draw back, push the sequin up in place and make a stitch on the edge of the sequin at the beginning of the previous stitch. Now make a stitch in the centre hole of the sequin and another stitch to the outer edge going forward. On the right side of the sequin there will be two threads over one half and one thread over the other half. The thread showing should not be unsightly but should be a good match to that of the sequin; alternatively, a fine metal thread could be used.

A combination of beads, bugles and sequins can be used on one piece of embroidery, the order in which they are worked varying with the design. If the idea is to have a bead line with draw back sequins either side, then the sequins will be worked first, with the beads worked second on top of the centre thread stitches from the sequins. Always endeavour to tambour the stand up beads and the fringe last of all on a piece of embroidery so that they will not impede any flat work. Thread and appliqué embroidery should be worked first, with the tambour beading worked second.

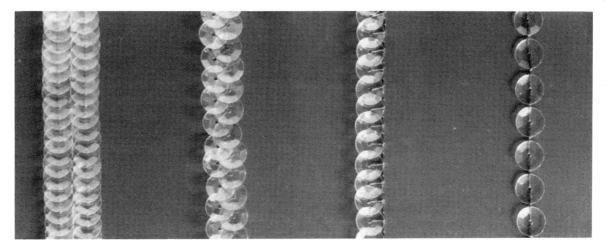

Figure 85 Sequins. (From left to right): Scaled sequins overlap each other; Zigzag; Draw back; Flat

Figure 86 Stand up sequins. Work over the ground shape with one bead and one stitch in the vermicelli pattern. Then work scaled sequins over the beads, filling in the design shape

Stand Up Sequins

For this technique, first work a spaced bead using one bead and one stitch in a ground cover, such as vermicelli. Then work the scaled sequins over the beads to the desired design shape. This method will stand the sequins up on one edge and they will be held in position by the beads previously worked. (Figure 86).

37. Wool

Wool for tambour work will have the chain or other stitches (Figure 87) used on the right side of the work. It is a quick technique as it is a thicker medium to work. A large needle will be required or a small crochet hook could be used; the same movement as for tambour will apply even if the latter is used. The large-hook needle will work satisfactorily on most fabrics; however, because the crochet hook has a blunt point this would be more satisfactory on a more loosely woven fabric. As this is a thicker medium the stitch length will need to be longer than when working with a fine thread. The pulled zigzag and the draw back could also be worked in wool, again with a larger stitch. A stepped draw back could produce a very interesting surface stitch; it could also have gradation of colour. This is worked by making the draw back stitch of the second line go through the centre of the stitches of the first line. A line of bugles could also be next to the lines of the wool to give a shine with the matt of the wool.

Figure 87 Wool chain stitch used for a counted thread design. The centre squares are worked using a draw back stitch pulled to the outside

Couching

Mohair, angora or other similar wools can easily be used with the couching technique. The wool is placed side by side, using three or four strands on the top of the fabric; they can be held in place with pins. Over the lines of wool work the draw back stitch; the vertical stitch must go over all the strands of the wool with the horizontal stitch in line with the strands of wool. Either a thread or fine metal thread can be used for the tambour stitch. A smooth wool or fancy wools can also be couched in this way; if it is a fine wool then more strands will be required for a wide draw back stitch. The use of zigzag stitch would give a slight wave effect to the wool. The cross zigzag would mean two rows of zigzag being worked, the second crossing the first row at the centre of each stitch. (Figure 88). Again, couching could easily be used with tambour beading to obtain an interesting effect with the shine and the matt. It will depend on the design as to whether the wool is worked first or last.

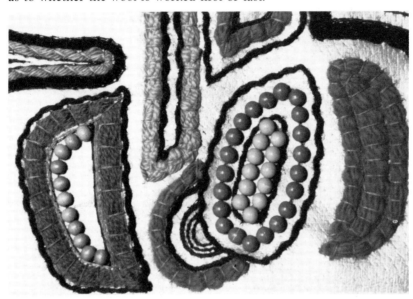

Figure 88 Couched wool and thread using the draw back and zigzag stitches. The beads are tamboured from the wrong side of the leather after all the couching has been completed

Fringe

The fringe is worked on the right side of the fabric by looping a multiple of long threads and stitching them at one edge only.

Make two tack lines, one for the top and one for the lower edge of the fringe. Fasten on just beneath the top line with a thread matching that of the fringe colour. The hanging fringe section could be worked with a variety of threads such as silk, thick cotton or wool. You can use a number of these threads together; the amount will depend on how thin or thick the finished fringe is required to be.

1. Lay the end of the fringe thread 2.5cm (1in) above the top tack line and to the right of the fastening on, then work a chain stitch over the fringe threads to the right. Make a small stitch, then chain back to the left.

2. Pin the longer end of the fringe threads to the lower tack line. Then take them back to lie by the side of the previous threads and above the top tack line working to the left.

3. Make a chain stitch over the fringe threads. Keep these top stitches in a straight line immediately below the top tack line.

4. Take the fringe threads to the left and make a draw back stitch over these threads to the top tack line.

5. Take the fringe down to the lower tack line and pin in position next to the previous loop. Make a chain stitch over the fringe threads just below the top tack line to the left.

6. Take the fringe threads back to the top to lie by the side of the previous fringe and above the top tack line.

7. Make a chain stitch over the fringe threads.

8. Take the fringe threads to the left and make the draw back stitch over these threads to the top tack line.

9. Take the fringe down to the lower tack line and pin in position next to the previous loop. Make a chain stitch over the fringe threads.

These movements are for two fringe loops each having three stitches holding the loops at the top. Continue these until completion; finish at the top tack line and leave a length of the fringe threads. The beginning and finish ends of the fringe are taken to the back and oversewn to the back of the work. (Figure 87).

Evenweave

Evenweave fabric can be worked upon to produce a variety of counted thread methods used for embroidery. The use of thread or wool and the counting of the threads of the fabric can produce a simulated blackwork by working the stitches to form a pattern. The pattern can be of different scales, different threads and filling areas, an outline of a shape such as Holbein stitch. (Figure 89).

The threads can be taken out of the evenweave for a drawn thread effect and stitches worked over the threads that remain. Draw back stitch on the edge of this simulates hemstitching. Chain stitch could pull the centre threads in different directions by working a number of rows. Use zigzag stitch over the threads for worked bars, and different threads could easily be used for a fine or heavy stitch line.

Figure 89 Blackwork using different scales of patterns with the chain for single and double lines

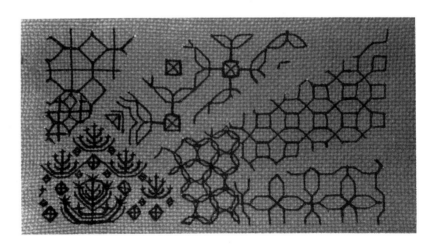

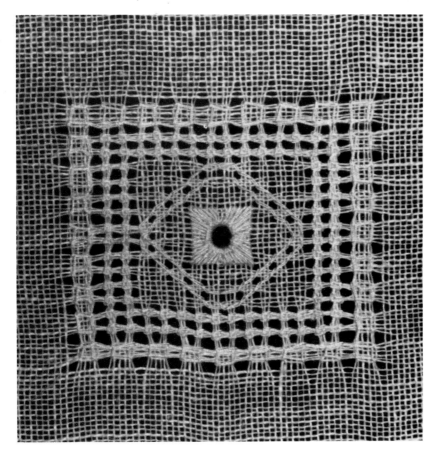

Figure 90 Drawn fabric using draw back stitches for the centre, zigzag for the diamond shape and chain for the outer squares

A loosely woven evenweave could easily be worked with simulated drawn fabric stitches. Use the stitch to pull the fabric threads together and so produce the decorative holes that form a pattern. Always use the stitches to their best advantage, such as working half the stitch in one direction and complete the other half of the stitch to produce the holes. Or work half the circles one way across and then complete the circles working back. For this the holes form the interest, therefore a fine thread should be used for the stitchery; however, a thicker thread could add more interest. Again, this will be determined by the required finished effect. (Figure 90).

Knitting

A fine or heavy piece of knitting can be used for tambour, and this could be machine or hand knitting.

If a fine knitting is being used it should be stretched and given a thorough press to form a square net. This can then be worked as for net previously described for either a fine outline or a solid filling. Alternatively, use the squares for blocking in by keeping to the squares rather than

Figure 91 Wool on knitting
using chain and draw back
stitches; this work will stretch
with the knitted background
fabric

working over them with a straight line. A mixture of threads from fine to
thick again can be used, or just one thread, throughout the execution of
these pieces of embroidery.

Heavy knitting would be better worked with a thick thread to give a
solid appearance by using the different stitches previously described.
However, if it is a heavy piece of knitting that has been knitted loosely it
could be pulled out to give a thick, square net fabric. This could then be
treated as for the net or pulled in different directions to produce even
larger holes. A combination could be built by working solid areas and
pulling the threads in different directions for larger holes. (Figure 91).

As well as producing variety with the stitching, fine and heavy knitting
could be combined easily while knitting the fabric by using a fine thread
and a chunky wool in a variety of ways. Then the tambour could be used
to produce some extremely interesting textures. It is always the desired
end product that governs the techniques that are to be employed.

Suppliers

U.K.

Machines

Singer
The Singer Company (U.K.) Ltd
15 Stanley Street
Cheetham
Manchester
M8 88H

Cornely
MEC (Sewing Machines) Ltd
15 Industrial Estate West
Witham
Essex
CM8 3BQ

G. Johnson & Sons Ltd
38 Riding House Street
London
W1P 7PL

Threads

William Hall & Co. Ltd
177 Stanley Road
Cheadle Hulme
Cheadle
Cheshire
SK8 6RF

Texere Yarns
9 Peckover Street
Bradford
West Yorkshire
BD1 5BD

Mace and Nairn
89 Crane Street
Salisbury
Wiltshire
SP1 2PY

J.H. Smith Ltd
Park Road
Calverton
Nottingham
NC14 6LL

Braid

Kersten Trimmings
87–95 Cleveland Street
London
W1P 5PW

Beads

Ells & Farrier Ltd
5 Princes Street
London W1
(also tambour holders
  and needles)

Cummins
64 Margaret Street
London W1

U.S.A.

Machines

Singer
The Singer Company
Stamford Forum
Stamford
Connecticut 06904

Threads

White Sewing Machine Group
Cleveland
Ohio 44111

American Thread Corporation
90 Park Avenue
New York

Yarn Depot
545 Sutter Street
San Francisco 95102

David Traum Inc.
West Paterson
New Jersey 07424

Beads and Sequins

Walbead Inc.
New York 10018

France

Machines

Cornely
9 Rue François Coppée
92–240 Malakoff

Index